THE INTERESTING HISTORY OF INCOME TAX

William J. Federer

★★ **Includes** ★★
U.S. PRESIDENT JOHN F. KENNEDY'S
TAX PLAN

THE INTERESTING HISTORY
HISTORY
OF
INCOME
TAX

William J. Federer

★★ Includes ★★
U.S. PRESIDENT JOHN F. KENNEDY'S
TAX PLAN

The Interesting History of Income Tax
by William J. Federer

To duplicate larger portions, please contact:

William J. Federer
P.O. Box 20163
St. Louis, MO 63123

314-487-4395
314-487-4489 fax
1-888-USA-WORD
wjfederer@gmail.com
www.amerisearch.net

HISTORY / EDUCATION ISBN 0-9753455-0-8

As owner of this book, you can take advantage of a limited-time
offer to get this book as a FREE EBOOK by simply emailing
wjfederer@gmail.com
and including in the subject line

Free Tax ebook

Amerisearch, Inc., P.O. Box 20163, St. Louis, MO 63123,
1-888-USA-WORD, 314-487-4395, 314-487-4489 fax
www.amerisearch.net, wjfederer@aol.com

To
my international tax attorney brother,
Richard E. Federer

TABLE
OF
CONTENTS

INTRODUCTION

On April 15, 1865, President Lincoln died. He was shot the night before in Ford's Theater.

On April 15, 1912, the Titanic sank. It struck an iceberg the night before.

And in 1954, April 15 became the deadline for filing Income Tax returns.

There has been much discussion on how to fix the tax system, but before that can happen, we must first have a basic understanding how we got here.

"It is time for a complete overhaul of our tax system. It is a disgrace to the human race," stated Jimmy Carter during his Democratic acceptance speech at Madison Square Garden, New York, 1976.[1]

Congressman J.C. Watts, Jr., serving as U.S. House Conference Chairman, responded to President Clinton's State of the Union Address in 1997:

> The American family is already overtaxed. Right now the average family spends about half of every dollar they earn in some type of government tax or government fee. Consider a 5-year-old child today.
>
> If things continue as they are, by the time they're 25 they'll pay about 84 cents of every dollar they make in some government tax or government fee. Friends, that's more than a shame, it's a scandal."[2]

The Internal Revenue Code has grown from 14 pages in 1913 to 2 volumes (6 inches thick) needing 8 volumes of Federal Tax Regulations to explain them.

In 1913, only the top 1 percent wealthiest people were required to file, now Americans pay nearly 30 percent of what they earn in Income Taxes.

According to The Tax Foundation, the average American has to work until April 17th to pay Federal, State and local taxes.

Some 8 billion pages of tax forms are sent out each year (using 300,000 trees!) requiring 7 billion man-hours to complete and file, which if fully compensated would cost taxpayers over $159 billion, equivalent to nearly 25 percent of what the IRS receives from those taxes.

Did our founders really intend to set up a government that would have to match up a billion 1099's with over a hundred million Form 1040's each year?[3]

FOUNDERS

America's founders were not fond of taxes.

When the French and Indian War ended in 1763, the British government imposed taxes on the American colonies to pay for their military defense.

These taxes and acts stifled the economy:

1760 Enforcement of Navigation Acts;
1760 Writs of Assistance empowering customs officers to search and confiscate private property at will;
1764 Currency Act;
1764 Sugar Act-taxing sugar, coffee, wine;
1765 Stamp Act-taxing newspapers, contracts, letters, playing cards and all printed materials;
1766 Declaratory Act;
1767 Townshend Acts-taxing glass, paints, paper.

In 1768, the British began quartering troops in American homes. When citizens gathered in protest, March 5, 1770, British soldiers fired into crowd killing five in what became called 'the Boston Massacre.'

Three years later, in 1773, the British passed another tax with the 'Tea Act.'

While American merchants paid taxes, British 'crony capitalism' allowed the East India Tea Company to sell a half million pounds of tea in the Colonies with no taxes, giving them a monopoly by underselling American merchants.

The citizens of Boston had enough.

On December 16, 1773, Sam Adams led a band of

patriots disguised as Mohawk Indians, called Sons of Liberty, from the South Meeting House to Griffin's Wharf. They boarded the ships *Dartmouth, Eleanor* and *Beaver,* and threw 342 chests of tea into the harbor.

This became called 'the Boston Tea Party.' The men of Marlborough, Massachusetts, declared:

> Death is more eligible than slavery. A free-born people are not required by the religion of Jesus Christ to submit to tyranny, but may make use of such power as God has given them to recover and support their liberties...
>
> We implore the Ruler above the skies that He would bare His arm...and let Israel go."

The Continental Congress passed Declaration and Resolves, October 14, 1774:

> Since the close of the last war, the British parliament, claiming a power...to bind the people of America by statutes in all cases whatsoever,
>
> hath...expressly imposed taxes on them...for the purpose of raising a revenue, hath imposed rates and duties...established a board of commissioners, with unconstitutional powers...not only for collecting the said duties, but for the trial of causes merely arising within the body of a county...
>
> Judges...have been made dependent on the crown alone for their salaries, and standing armies kept in times of peace...
>
> All which statutes are impolitic, unjust, and cruel, as well as unconstitutional, and most dangerous and destructive of American rights...
>
> The inhabitants of the English colonies in North-America...

Resolved...That they are entitled to life, liberty and property: and they have never ceded to any foreign power whatever, a right to dispose of either without their consent....

Resolved...That the foundation of English liberty, and of all free government, is a right in the people to participate in their legislative council: and as the English colonists are not represented...in the British parliament, they are entitled to a free and exclusive power of legislation in their several provincial legislatures...in all cases of taxation and internal polity...

We...consent to the operation of such acts of the British parliament, as are bonafide, restrained to the regulation of our external commerce...excluding every idea of taxation internal or external, for raising a revenue on the subjects, in America, without their consent."

Isaac Backus was a delegate to the Massachusetts Convention which ratified the U.S. Constitution. He was a Baptist minister and a founder of Brown University. Isaac Backus addressed the Massachusetts Assembly in 1775:

Is not all America now appealing to Heaven against the injustice of being taxed...

We are persuaded that an entire freedom from being taxed by civil rulers...is not mere favor from any men in the world but a right and property granted us by God, who commands us to stand fast in it.[4]

The Declaration, July 4, 1776, listed taxes as one of the reason America wanted independence:

The history of the present King of Great Britain is a history of repeated injuries and usurpations, all having in direct object the establishment of an absolute tyranny over these States...

He has...giv[en] assent to their acts of pretended legislation... for imposing taxes on us without our consent.[5]

The patriots' rallying cry was "no taxation without representation."

Beginning in 1777, the Articles of Confederation served as the government in the United States. These Articles did not grant the Federal government any power to tax, leaving the taxing power solely under "the authority and direction of the legislatures of the several States."[6]

∽

FIRST MOTIVATION FOR TAXES

In 1787, the U.S. Constitution was approved, acknowledging the first motivation for taxes - TO PAY FOR LEGITIMATE GOVERNMENT EXPENDITURES, such as roads, canals, paying debts and providing for an army and navy.

These were paid for with tariff taxes on imports, called duties or imposts, and excise taxes on specific items such as carriages, distilled spirits, tobacco, sugar, and salt.

The U.S. Constitution (Article I, Section 8.1) made provision:

> To lay and collect taxes, duties, imposts, and excises to pay the debts and provide for the common defense and general welfare of the United States.[8]

The U.S. Constitution prohibited a Federal income tax (Article 1, Section 9.4):

> No capitation or other direct tax shall be laid, unless in proportion to the census or enumeration hereinbefore directed to be taken.[9]

In the 1790's, the Federalist Party added excise taxes on houses, lands, stamps, voting at polls, and numerous other items, but this slowed economic growth and reduced tax revenue. Resistance to these taxes led to the Whiskey Rebellion of 1794.

In 1802, President Jefferson repealed excise taxes on everything except salt. This, along with revenue from the sale of western lands, resulted in a significant surplus. In his First Inaugural Address, March 4, 1801, Jefferson admonished:

> Adoring an overruling Providence, which by all its dispensations proves that it delights in the happiness of man here and his greater happiness hereafter.
>
> With all these blessings, what more is necessary to make us a happy and prosperous people? Still one thing more, fellow citizens - a wise and frugal Government, which shall restrain men from injuring one another, shall leave them otherwise free to regulate their own pursuits of industry and improvement, and shall not take from the mouth of labor the bread it has earned.

Jefferson observed an inverse relationship:
-HIGHER TAXES slowed the economy resulting
in reduced tax revenue to the government.
-LOWER TAXES helped the economy to expand,
bringing more tax revenue into the government.

In other words, it is better to have a smaller percentage
of a larger amount of money changing hands than a larger
percentage of a small amount of money changing hands.

Montesquieu wrote in *The Spirit of the Laws*, 1752:

> The effect of excessive taxes is slavery;
> and slavery produces a diminution of tribute...
> (Byzantine Emperor) Anastasius invented
> a tax for breathing.

Jefferson wrote in his 2nd Annual Message, 1802:

> We are able, without a direct tax, without
> internal taxes, and without borrowing, to make
> large and effectual payments toward the discharge
> of our public debt and the emancipation of our
> posterity from that mortal canker.
> It is an encouragement, fellow-citizens,
> of the highest order to proceed as we have begun
> in substituting economy for taxation.[10]

Jefferson was not in favor of taxing some more
than others, as he wrote to Joseph Milligan, April 6, 1816,
Prospectus on Political Economy:

> Perfection of the function of taxation...[is]
> to do equal and impartial justice to all...
> To take from one, because it is thought
> that his own industry and that of his fathers has
> acquired too much, in order to spare to others,

who, or whose fathers have not exercised equal industry and skill, is to violate arbitrarily the first principle of association, 'the guarantee to every one of a free exercise of his industry, and the fruits acquired by it.'

In his 2nd Inaugural Address, Jefferson spoke of cutting taxes and eliminating "unnecessary offices" and "useless establishments":

These covering our land with officers, and opening our doors to intrusions, had already begun that process of domiciliary vexation which, once entered, is scarcely to be restrained from reaching successfully every article of produce and property.

During the War of 1812, taxes were re-imposed to pay for the war. Afterward they were repealed, again resulting in the economy growing and tax revenues increasing. President Jackson warned December 5, 1836:

Congress is only authorized to levy taxes 'to pay the debts and provide for the common defense and general welfare of the United States.'
There is no such provision as would authorize Congress to collect together the property of the country, under the name of revenue, for the purpose of dividing it equally or unequally among the States or the people. Indeed, it is not probable that such an idea ever occurred to the States when they adopted the Constitution...
No people can hope to perpetuate their liberties who long acquiesce in a policy which taxes them for objects not necessary to the legitimate and real wants of their Government...

The practical effect of such an attempt must ever be to burden the people with taxes, not for the purposes beneficial to them, but to swell the profits of deposit banks and support a band of useless public officers... There would soon be but one taxing power, and that vested in a body of men far removed from the people...

The States...would not dare to murmur at the proceedings of the General Government, lest they should lose their supplies; all would be merged in a practical consolidation, cemented by widespread corruption, which could only be eradicated by one of those bloody revolutions which occasionally overthrow the despotic systems of the Old World.[18]

SECOND MOTIVATION FOR TAXES

Soon, Congress discovered a second motivation for taxes - ECONOMIC ENGINEERING, where taxes were used to help some industries and hurt others.

Supreme Court Chief Justice John Marshall stated in *McCulloch vs. Maryland*, 1819:

The power to tax involves the power to destroy.[19]

Jefferson acknowledged this to Joseph Milligan, April 6, 1816, *Prospectus on Political Economy*:

How far it may be the interest and the duty of all to submit to this sacrifice...to pay for a time an impost on the importation of certian articles, in order to encourage their manufacture at home, or an excise on others injurious to the morals or health of the citizens, will depend on a series of considerationas...but when decided, and the principle settled, it is to be equally and fairly applied to all.

For example, tariff taxes on imports from European countries made them more expensive, thus discouraging Americans from buying them.

On the other hand, lower taxes on American-made products made them less expensive, encouraging people to buy them, thus helping American industries grow.

This is the reasoning behind 'sin' taxes, where liquor, cigarettes, tobacco, etc., are taxed to make them more expensive and thereby discourage people from buying them.

President Jackson opposed excessive taxation, stating in a Veto Message, 1830:

Through the favor of an overruling and indulgent Providence our country is blessed with general prosperity and our citizens exempted from the pressure of taxation, which other less favored portions of the human family are obliged to bear.[20]

President Jackson stated in his Farewell Address, 1837:

There is, perhaps, no one power conferred on the Federal Government so liable to abuse as the taxing power...

Plain as these principles appear to be, you

will yet find there is a constant effort to induce the General Government to go beyond the limits of its taxing power and to impose unnecessary burdens upon the people...to fasten upon the people this unjust and unequal system.[22]

But still, there was no Federal income tax, as President Franklin Pierce stated December 5, 1853:

Happily, I have no occasion to suggest any radical changes in the financial policy of the Government. Ours is almost, if not absolutely, the solitary power of Christendom having a surplus revenue drawn immediately from imposts on commerce.[23]

WARTIME INCOME TAXES

Before the Civil War, nearly 90 percent of the Federal Government's revenue came from tariff taxes on imports, mostly collected from Southern ports, like Charleston, South Carolina.

The tariff taxes that helped the North hurt the South, as the South had no factories to protect.

This was a source of animosity leading up to the Civil War.

The Southern economy was agricultural, mostly cotton and rice, which deplorably relied on slave labor.

Less than two months after Lincoln was sworn in,

South Carolina threatened to stop collecting tariffs, as their economy was experiencing a severe downturn.

Lincoln sent troops to the Federal Fort Sumter in Charleston's harbor.

Confederate General P.G.T. Beauregard fired upon the fort, April 12, 1861, beginning the Civil War.

In this national emergency, the Federal Government imposed the first income tax on the United States.

The North financed the war with $750 million raised through taxes, $450 million by printing greenbacks and $3 billion from loans.

The Bureau of Internal Revenue was created in 1862 and taxed all incomes:

> Whether derived from any kind of property, rents, interest, dividends, salaries, or from any trade, employment or vocation carried on in the United States or elsewhere, or from any source whatever.[24]

Incomes under $600 were not taxed, incomes from $600 to $10,000 (equivalent to $12,000 to $250,000 today) were taxed at a mere 3 percent, and incomes over $10,000 were taxed at 5 percent.

Just as taxes were raised during the War of 1812, John Steele Gordon, in his article "American Taxation" (*American Heritage*, May 1996), noticed that during the Civil War a principle of taxation was observed, namely that:

> People will willingly pay very high taxes during wartime.[25]

THIRD MOTIVATION FOR INCOME TAXES

The third motivation for taxes - SOCIAL ENGINEERING, epitomized in Karl Marx's line:

"From each according to his ability; to each according to his need." (*Critique of the Gotha Programme*, 1875; also in U.S.S.R. Constitution, 1936, Article 1426.)

After the Civil War, General Ulysses S. Grant became the youngest U.S. President to that date, being 46 years old. President Grant responded to the cry for relief from overburdened citizens by completely repealing the Federal Income Tax in 1873.

This, along the Colorado Gold Rush and increased protective tariffs, caused the economy of the North to grow at an unprecedented rate. A friend of Grant's, author Mark Twain, labeled this era the "Gilded Age." America saw:

-Immigrants arriving in record numbers;
-Iron, steel production rising dramatically;
-Railroads crossing the nation;
-Western resources of lumber, gold and silver being tapped;
-Oil industry replacing the use of whale blubber oil, saving the whale;
-Industry and manufacturing expanding quickly, providing labor-saving household appliances to the masses, freeing especially women from time spent on domestic duties.

Industrialists, aided by protective tariffs, helped provide more goods to more people at cheaper prices than at any previous time in world history. There was an unprecedented rise in the standard of living.

Unfortunately, Presidents Grant's military training of trusting subordinates left him ill-prepared for dealing with political intrigues, hidden motives, and greed of Washington politicians.

As a result, a number of those in his Administration were involved in granting government favors and monopolies in exchange for bribes and insider deals.

At the same time America's standard of living skyrocketed, new industrialists amassed enormous fortunes:

John Jacob Astor (real estate, fur);
Andrew Carnegie (steel);
James Fisk (finance);
Henry Flagler (railroads, oil);
Jay Gould (railroads);
Edward Harriman (railroads);
Andrew Mellon (finance, oil);
J.P. Morgan (finance, industrial);
John D. Rockefeller (oil);
Charles M. Schwab (steel); and
Cornelius Vanderbilt (water transport, railroads).

Some industrialists began to be derogatorily labeled 'robber barons' as complaints arose from unsafe working facilities, child-labor, low wages, accidents and occasionally slave-labor type conditions in factories.

Though many industrialists genuinely sought to provide well for their employees, others justified their position at the top of the economic ladder as evidence of Darwin's 'survival of the fittest' theory, calling it 'social Darwinism.'

On the other side of the world, Darwin's theory was adapted by Karl Marx into a 'class-struggle' to redistribute wealth. Marx wanted to organize the working class, whom he called 'the proletariat', and incite them to revolt against business and property owners, whom he called 'bourgeoisie'.

Marx's *Communist Manifesto* (1847) advocated overthrowing the capitalist class with a world-wide working-class revolution, adapting Hegel's dialectic tactic to foment political unrest. Labor organizers and community organizers were sent into communities for the purpose of creating crises. They would play upon the greed of the poor and stir them to riot, thereby disrupting social order so that communists could seize control.

Forty-five countries fell to communism through this method. Marx wrote:

> The theory of the Communists may be summed up in the single sentence: Abolition of private property.[27]

Marx's philosophy influenced America's Western and Southern States with the Populist and Granger movements, and Eastern States with the Labor and Union movements. Marx proposed the government take from rich 'exploiters' and give to poor 'exploited' in a sort of officially-sanctioned theft program, thus matching the greed of the industrialists with the greed of the masses.

Certain politicians embraced this theory, such Senator John Sherman, who argued:

> Here we have in New York Mr. Astor with an income of millions...and we have alongside of him a poor man receiving $1,000 a year... and yet we are afraid to tax the income of Mr. Astor.

Is there any justice in it? Why, sir, the
income tax is the only one that tends to equalize
these burdens between the rich and the poor.[28]

Felix Adler, founder of the Ethical Culture
movement, suggested a 100 percent tax on income above
the amount required: "to supply all the comforts and true
refinements of life."[29]

Unfortunately, wherever Marx's philosophy was put
into practice, those in charge of 'redistributing' wealth
inevitably yielded to the temptation to 'redistribute' it to
those who could helpthem stay in power.

Instead of equality, this produced greater inequality
and corrupt political favoritism, controlled by a despotic
political boss.

It dis-incentivized production and innovation,
reduced the standard of living, restricted freedom, and led
to dictatorships responsible for over 100 million deaths.

Franklin Roosevelt identified communism as
simply repackaged dictatorship when he addressed the
American Youth Congress, February 10, 1940:

The Soviet Union...is run by a dictatorship
as absolute as any other dictatorship in the world.

The Soviet Union understood the 'social
engineering' effect of taxes.

Communist leader Vladimir Lenin viewed middle-
class business owners, 'bourgeoisie', as a threat to
centralized government, therefore he implemented 'social
engineering' policies to eliminate them. Lenin stated:

The way to crush the bourgeoisie is to
grind them between the millstones of taxation and
inflation.

Taxes intentionally took away money from potential tea-party type 'anti-revolutionaries'; and inflation evaporated any money they had saved up.

This way, citizens were forced to spend every waking hour worrying about what to eat that night, leaving them with no time or resources to plot an overthrow the communist government.

In a manner similar to how Ottoman Turks controlled their non-Turkish subjects, Josef Stalin in the Soviet Union added another control tactic - fear.

The cliché 'fear and food' described how citizens were prevented from challenging the government's power by continual food shortages which forced them to remain dependent on government rationing; and also by the fear of being dragged away in the night by government agents.

SOCIAL ENGINEERING'S EFFECT ON CHURCHES

Back in America, the U.S. Government's experiment in social engineering had an unforeseen consequence - it encroached upon the churches' traditional role of caring for the needs of the poor.

Catholic and Protestant churches started hospitals, medical clinics, cared for maimed soldiers, prisoners, unwed mothers, orphans, widows, shut-ins, homeless, juvenile delinquents, immigrants, provided charitable social services such as schools, soup kitchens, feeding of the poor, welfare, and benevolence.

Churches also helped maintain a virtuous, responsible populace, which reduced crime, child abuse, derelicts, and other social ills, which would otherwise be immense financial burdens on society.

In the early 1800's, evangelist Charles Finney had formed the Benevolent Empire, a network of volunteer organizations to aid poor and aged with healthcare and social needs, which, by 1834, had a budget rivaling the Federal Government.

Charles Finney's revival preaching inspired George Williams to found the YMCA in 1844, and William and Catherine Booth to found The Salvation Army in 1865.

Though well-intentioned, the Government began to usurp the role of caring for the poor away from churches.

As government programs were implemented to help the poor, another factor became evident. People tended to vote for those who gave them benefits. This tempted politicians to redirect government funds into projects and programs intended not so much to help the poor as to help the politicians get reelected.

Sir Alexander Tytler described this temptation in the democracy of Athens in his book, *Universal History from the Creation of the World to the Beginning of the 18th Century* (Boston: Fetridge & Co., 1834; 1850):

> The senate was, in theory, a wise institution...but...being annually elected, its members were ever under the necessity of courting that people for their votes, and of flattering their prejudices and passions, by adopting and proposing measures which had no other end than to render themselves popular...
>
> The guardians nominally of the people's rights, they were themselves the abject slaves of a corrupted populace...

> They were perpetually quarreling about the limits of authority, and instead of a salutary and cordial cooperation for the general good of the state, it was an eternal contest for supremacy, and a mutual desire of each other's abasement...
>
> They were perpetually divided into factions, which servilely ranked themselves under the banners of the contending demagogues; and these maintained their influence over their partisans by the most shameful corruption and bribery, of which the means were supplied alone by the plunder of the public money.

The 'social engineering' impact of taxation is always present, whether intentional or not.

Author's anecdotal stories: Running for Congress years ago I went door-to-door introducing myself and stating some campaign issues, including repealing the 'marriage penalty' where married couples paid taxes at a higher rate than single individuals.

At one house a teenager answered the door, followed by his parents. When I mentioned repealing the 'marriage penalty', the teenager chuckled and walked away. When inquiring if I said something wrong, the father responded: "No, that's just the reason we are not married. We save thousands of dollars a year on our taxes by filing as two single individuals rather than as a married couple."

At another house, when I mentioned repealing the 'marriage penalty' a woman started crying, saying her boyfriend refused to marry her because they would have to pay thousands more in taxes.

A tremendous financial burden is imposed on local, State and Federal Government budgets due to the ripple effect of broken homes, such as increased welfare dependency, delinquency, gang violence, crime, incarcerations, larger police budgets, property damage, insurance rates, and more.

It would be to society's benefit to 'social engineer' an incentive for stable marriages and families. One suggestion would be, instead of a marriage penalty, offer an increased tax deduction for each year a couple stayed married.

PEACETIME INCOME TAXES

In 1894, the Democrat controlled Congress passed the first peacetime income tax. It was a 2 percent tax on incomes over $4,000 ($80,000 today).

As only 85,000 out of 12 million people had incomes over $4,000 in 1894, the tax was only on the top 1 percent wealthiest individuals in the country.

In 1895, the United States Supreme Court declared income tax unconstitutional in *Pollock v. Farmers' Loan and Trust Co.* Chief Justice Melville W. Fuller understood income tax to exist only during wartime:

> The original expectation was that the power of direct taxation would be exercised only in extraordinary exigencies, and down to August 15, 1894, this expectation has been realized.[30]

Justice Stephen J. Field concurred:

> The income tax law under consideration... discriminates between those who receive an income of four thousand dollars and those who

do not... The legislation, in the discrimination it makes, is class legislation.

Whenever a distinction is made in the burdens a law imposes or in the benefits it confers on any citizens by reason of their birth, or wealth, or religion, it is class legislation, and leads inevitably to oppression and abuses, and to general unrest and disturbance in society...

Justice Field continued:

It was hoped and believed that the great amendments to the Constitution which followed the late civil war had rendered such legislation impossible for all future time.

But the objectional legislation reappears in the act under consideration.

It is the same in essential character as that of the English income statute of 1691, which taxed Protestants at a certain rate, Catholics, as a class, at double the rate of Protestants, and Jews at another and separate rate.[31]

Theodore Roosevelt saw how industrialists were creating monopolies and trying to gain control of the banking system. Roosevelt stated April 14, 1908:

Already the evils of monopoly are becoming manifest.[33]

Standard Oil Company's John D. Rockefeller made under-the-table agreements with railroad companies to ship his oil cheaper than his competitors. Rockefeller would then sell his oil cheaper and put his competitors out of business.

Once Rockefeller had a monopoly, he would raise the price of oil very high, making enough profit to pay back the railroads. Roosevelt told Congress, May 4, 1906:

> Thus in New England the refusal of certain railway systems to prorate has resulted in keeping the Standard Oil in absolute monopolistic control of the field, enabling it to charge from three to four hundred thousand dollars a year more to the consumers of oil in New England than they would have had to pay had the price paid been that obtaining in the competitive fields...
>
> This is a characteristic example of the numerous evils which are inevitable under a system in which the big shipper and the railroad are left free to crush out all individual initiative.[34]

Conjuring images of the modern-day wealth of globalists, Roosevelt responded that wealthy industrialists should be subject to an inheritance tax to prevent the "transmission in their entirety of those fortunes swollen beyond all healthy limits."[32]

Theodore Roosevelt stated December 3, 1906:

> An income tax stands on an entirely different footing from an inheritance tax; because it involves no question of the perpetuation of fortunes swollen to an unhealthy size."[35]

Theodore Roosevelt stated December 3, 1907:

> No advantage comes either to the country as a whole or to the individuals inheriting the money by permitting the transmission in their entirety of the enormous fortunes which would be affected by such a tax.[36]

The President after Theodore Roosevelt was William Taft. Taft yielded to the mounting public pressure to tax the rich by placing a 2 percent tax on corporate profits, as only the wealthy owned corporate stock.

Taft instituted this 'income tax' by creatively calling it an 'excise tax', June 16, 1909:

> The decision in the Pollock case left power in the National Government to levy an excise tax which accomplishes the same purpose as a corporation income tax...
>
> I therefore recommend an amendment to the tariff bill imposing upon all corporations and joint stock companies for profit...an excise tax measured by 2 per cent on the net income of such corporations...
>
> This is an excise tax upon the privilege of doing business as an artificial entity and of freedom from a general partnership liability enjoyed by those who own the stock.[37]

The next President, Woodrow Wilson, believed that tariff taxes on imports between countries caused wars. With World War I threatening, Wilson naively thought that if he could reduce tariff taxes it would pacify tensions between countries and bring about world peace.

As tariffs were the main source of revenue for the Federal Government, Wilson proposed replacing them with an income tax on the rich.

The U.S. Senate, a quarter of whom were millionaires, realized public opinion would prevail, so they switched from being against the income tax to voting in favor of it 77-0, then quickly passed legislation creating tax shelters so they could avoid paying it.

The 16th Amendment, 1913, stated:

Congress shall have the power to lay and
collect taxes on incomes, from whatever sources
derived, without apportionment among the several
States, and without regard to any census or
enumeration.[38]

The original 1913 IRS Form 1040 only taxed the
top 1 percent of Americans at a rate of only 1 percent.

Specifically, it was a tax of 1 percent tax on incomes
over $3,000 (around $100,000 today), with a $1,000
marital deduction, and a top rate of 7 percent tax on
incomes over $500,000. At these rates, 99 percent of
Americans were exempt.

᠙

501(C)3 CHURCHES

Prior to 1913, churches did not have to worry
about 'losing their IRS tax-exempt status' as there was no
IRS. When Congress created the IRS, it had a 501(c)3
category for "religious, educational, or charitable
purposes":

1) exempting them from paying taxes; and
2) allowing tax deductions for contributors.

This tradition can be traced back to England's 1601
Elizabethan Statute of Charitable Uses (43 Eliz. 1, C4):

For relief of aged, impotent and poor
people, some for maintenance of sick and maimed

soldiers and mariners, schools of learning, free schools and scholars in universities, some for repair of bridges, ports, havens, causeways, churches, sea-banks, and highways, some for education and preferment of orphans, some for marriages of poor maids, some for supportation, aid and help of young tradesmen, handicraftsmen, and persons decayed; and others for relief or redemption of prisoners or captives, and for aid or ease of any poor inhabitants."

501(C)3 ROBBER BARONS

As other organizations wanted to avoid taxes, the religious church category grew to include:

1913 - Organizations for scientific purposes;
1918 - Organizations for the prevention of cruelty to children or animals;
1921 - Corporations and community chest funds;
1921 - Organizations testing for literacy;
1954 - Organizations testing for public safety;
1976 - Organizations to foster national or international amateur sports competition.

Many find it odd that churches are in the same IRS category as foundations to foster amateur sports competitions.

Wealthy individuals, such as John D. Rockefeller- the richest man in the world at the time, Andrew Carnegie-the second richest man in the world, Henry Ford, and others, used the 501(c)3 category to create foundations into which they could transfer their assets to avoid taxes yet still direct the use of their funds, ie. Rockefeller Foundation, Carnegie Foundation, Ford Foundation, etc.

They also helped create tax-exempt state and local bonds, and exclusions for gifts, life insurance proceeds.

501(C)3 COMMUNISTS

After Russia's Bolshevik Revolution in 1917, Communist agitators spread to other countries, including the United States. Communist leaning groups began forming 501(c)3 educational foundations in order to pamphleteer, work as community organizers and recruit into labor unions to promote their agenda.

To limit their anti-American activity, Congress passed the Espionage Act of 1917 and Sedition Act of 1918.

In 1919, the Communist Party USA was founded.

In response, the U.S. Treasury Department argued in 1919 that foundations "formed to disseminate controversial or partisan propaganda" could not be considered "educational" 501(c)3 foundations.

In 1920, a World War I draft-dodger named Roger Baldwin, together with socialist and communist anti-war protesters, founded a 501(c)3 foundation called the ACLU to defend those accused of communist activities.

In 1923, Roger Baldwin's friend, Margaret Sanger,

founded a 501(c)3 organization that became Planned Parenthood to implement a eugenic plan to eliminate 'human weeds'. She was supported by the Rockefeller and Carnegie Foundations.

During this time, churches continued the American tradition of helping the poor and speaking out politically.

Many Protestant churches spoke out in the 1928 Presidential Election in opposition of Governor Al Smith of New York, who was campaigning to become the nation's first Catholic President.

This was repeated in 1960 with candidate John F. Kennedy, a Catholic, running for President.

In the 1934 Revenue Act, Congress further restricted many 501(c)3 foundations from influencing legislation by 'substantial' lobbying, though the term 'substantial' was never defined.

Though most churches were not 'corporations' for religious purposes, the IRS began to treat them as if they had incorporated.

Pastors and churches lost more freedom when Democrat Senator Lyndon B. Johnson was running for reelection to the Senate in Texas.

Some educational 501(c)3 organizations were letting constituents know about LBJ's big government positions, accusing him of being communist-leaning.

An example was an article titled "The Texas Story" written by Willis Ballinger (*Spotlight for the Nation*, No. D-269), which was circulated in 1954 by the 501(c)3 Committee for Constitutional Government.

Willis Ballinger wrote, as cited in Mark Eldon Young's 1993 University of Texas Masters Thesis - 'Lyndon B. Johnson's Forgotten Campaign: Re-election to the Senate in 1954':

A vote for Johnson - many Texans feel -

will be a vote for more centralization of power and socialism in Washington; for more of the internationalism which is designed to abolish the U.S.A.; and for more covering up of Communist infiltration.

As his re-election approached, Johnson grew more nervous and pursued ways to silence the 501(c)3's which criticized him, especially the FACTS FORUM and the Committee for Constitutional Government.

On July 2, 1954. LBJ introduced a tax code change further limiting what 501(c)3's could do politically.

TAXES, OUTSOURCING & JOB LOSS

The original income tax was sold to the public as a 'soak-the-rich' tax. Average citizens never imagined that the income tax would someday tax them.

The income tax moved investment capital away from creating jobs and into efforts to shelter capital in non-profit corporations.

Theoretically, since the income tax was a 'direct' tax on the incomes of the wealthy, the 'indirect' taxes on inheritances and corporations should have been repealed.

The satisfaction the low and middle-class enjoyed in getting the wealthy to 'pay their fair share' was short-lived. Soon the wartime emergency of World War I, as with the Civil War, saw income taxes extended to nearly the entire population.

It was a 4 percent tax on incomes over $1,000 ($30,000 today), with a $1,000 marital deduction ($50,000 today), with up to a 13 percent tax on high incomes.

After the World War I, income taxes were reduced, and again the economy grew and tax revenues increased from $690 million to $711 million. In 1920, only 13 percent of the labor force paid income taxes, filing 5.5 million returns.

During this time of the 'roaring twenties', President Calvin Coolidge stated May 31, 1926:

> While many other nations...are struggling with a burden of increased debts and rising taxes, which makes them seek for new sources from which by further taxation they can secure new revenues, we have made large toward paying off our national debt, have greatly reduced our national taxes, and been able to relieve the people by abandoning altogether many sources of national revenue.[40]

During the Great Depression in the 1930's, Franklin D. Roosevelt instituted a 'Wealth Tax' which drove enormous amounts of money out of American jobs and manufacturing into tax shelters.

Franklin Roosevelt then followed the precedent of the Civil War and World War I by expanding the Federal income tax with "the greatest tax bill in American history." The Revenue Act of 1942 raised the income tax rate to 6 percent.

In 1943, Congress passed the 'Pay-As-You-Go' tax where employers withheld taxes from employees' paychecks as an emergency way to get money to fight Hitler. It was part of the patriotic war enthusiasm which included slogans such as:

'UNCLE SAME NEEDS YOU';
'BUY WAR BONDS'; and
'SMASH THE AXIS-PAY YOUR TAXES.'

The Federal Government would forgive people for not paying their annual lump sum taxes at the end of 1941 if they signed up to have future taxes withheld from each paycheck.

The idea of withholding taxes came from Beardsley Ruml, treasurer of Macy's Department Store who became Chairman of the Federal Reserve Bank of New York.

Ruml was helped by Bernard Baruch and Milton Friedman. So much money came in from the 'Pay-As-You-Go' tax with so few complaints that it continued after the war. President John F. Kennedy stated April 20, 1961:

> Our system of combined withholding and voluntary reporting on wages and salaries under the individual income tax has served us well...
>
> Introduced during the war when the income tax was extended to millions of new taxpayers, the wage-withholding system has been one of the most important and successful advances in our tax system in recent times...
>
> Initial difficulties were quickly overcome, and the new system helped the taxpayer no less than the tax collector.[45]

Kennedy continued:

> In meeting the demands of war finance, the individual income tax moved from a selective tax imposed on the wealthy to the means by which the great majority of our citizens participate in

paying for well over one-half of our total budget receipts."[39]

After World War II, America rebuilt factories in Germany and Japan under the Marshall Plan. Businesses soon discovered they could build factories overseas and ship goods back to America, thus avoiding corporate income taxes. They would then lobby to reduce tariff taxes on imports.

Businesses manufacturing on America soil were placed at a disadvantage. Increasing taxes had the consequence of not just channeling money into unproductive tax-free foundations, but driving investment capital and jobs out of the country.

Kennedy stated November 20, 1962:

> Our present tax system...exerts too heavy a drag on growth... It reduces the financial incentives for personal effort, investment, and risk-taking... The present...tax load...distorts economic judgments and channels an undue amount of energy into efforts to avoid tax liabilities.[43]

Squeeze the sponge and the water flows out. Investment dollars and jobs flowed to other countries due to the anti-business squeeze of:

-Higher Taxes;
-Higher Wages & Benefits;
-More Lawsuits;
-Increased Government Bureaucracy
-Environmental Protection Agency restrictions; and
-'Crony Capitalism' or 'Corporate Welfare' where companies supporting the politicians in

power received favoritism and those not supporting them did not.

To stay competitive in the global marketplace, many businesses were faced with the choice: GO OUT OF THE COUNTRY or GO OUT OF BUSINESS!

Microsoft founder Bill Gates acknowledged this problem in an interview on MSNBC's Morning Joe, January 21, 2014. When asked by co-host Mika Brzezinski if he supported raising the minimum wage, Bill Gates responded:

> Well, jobs are a great thing. So you have to be a bit careful: If you raise the minimum wage, you're encouraging labor substitution, and you're going to go buy machines and automate things - or cause jobs to appear outside of that jurisdiction...
> And so within certain limits, you know, it does cause job destruction. If you really start pushing it, then you're just making a huge trade-off.

Bill Gates addressed the American Enterprise Institute, March 13, 2014, warning of job loss:

> Software substitution, whether it's for drivers or waiters or nurses - it's progressing...
> Technology over time will reduce demand for jobs, particularly at the lower end of skill set. 20 years from now, labor demand for lots of skill sets will be substantially lower. I don't think people have that in their mental model...
> When people say we should raise the minimum wage. I worry about what that does to job creation - potentially damping demand in the part of the labor spectrum that I'm most worried about.

The trend of outsourcing produced an additional effect, namely, the diminishing of patriotic attachment in those companies moving overseas.

This gave rise to a category of financial 'globalists' whose loyalty was to bottom line on their Profit and Loss statements. When President Kennedy became aware of outsourcing, he stated February 6, 1961:

> I have asked the Secretary of the Treasury to report by April 1 on whether present tax laws may be stimulating in undue amounts the flow of American capital to the industrial countries abroad through special preferential treatment.[41]

Kennedy reiterated April 20, 1961:

> In those countries where income taxes are lower than in the United States, the ability to defer the payment of U.S. tax by retaining income in the subsidiary companies provides a tax advantage for companies operating through overseas subsidiaries that is not available to companies operating solely in the United States.
>
> Many American investors properly made use of this deferral in the conduct of their foreign investment.[42]

Kennedy stated January 23, 1963:

> The present tax codes...inhibit the mobility and formation of capital, add complexities and inequities which undermine the morale of the taxpayer, and make tax avoidance rather than market factors a prime consideration in too many economic decisions.[44]

The answer to the outsourcing problem is simple - make it more profitable to have factories located here than there!

ᕰ

KENNEDY'S STIMULUS PLAN - REDUCE TAXES

Kennedy stated September 18, 1963:

> The high wartime and postwar tax rates we are now paying are no longer necessary. They are, in fact, harmful. These high rates do not leave enough money in private hands to keep this country's economy growing and healthy.

Kennedy's stimulus plan was to keep jobs in America by reducing taxes, stating January 17, 1963:

> Lower rates of taxation will stimulate economic activity and so raise the levels of personal and corporate income as to yield within a few years an increased - not a reduced - flow of revenues to the Federal Government.[12]

Kennedy stated, November 20, 1962:

> It is a paradoxical truth that tax rates are too high and tax revenues are too low... Cutting taxes now is not to incur a budget deficit, but to achieve the more prosperous, expanding economy which can bring a budget surplus."[11]

Kennedy stated January 21, 1963:

>   In today's economy, fiscal prudence and responsibility call for tax reduction even if it temporarily enlarges the Federal deficit - why reducing taxes is the best way open to us to increase revenues...
>   It is no contradiction - the most important single thing we can do to stimulate investment in today's economy is to raise consumption by major reduction of individual income tax rates.[13]

Kennedy told Congress, January 24, 1963:

>   Our tax system still siphons out of the private economy too large a share of personal and business purchasing power and reduces the incentive for risk, investment and effort - thereby aborting our recoveries and stifling our national growth rate.[15]

Kennedy stated on his Tax Reduction Bill, September 18, 1963:

>   A tax cut means higher family income and higher business profits and a balanced Federal budget. Every taxpayer and his family will have more money left over after taxes for a new car, a new home, new conveniences, education, and investment.
>   Every businessman can keep a higher percentage of his profits in his cash register or put it to work expanding or improving his business, and as the national income grows, the Federal Government will ultimately end up with more revenues.[15]

Kennedy continued:

> Prosperity is the real way to balance our budget. Our tax rates are so high today that the growth of profits and pay checks in this country have been stunted.
>
> Our tax revenues have been depressed and our books for out of the last 10 years have been in the red. By lowering tax rates, by increasing jobs and income, we can expand tax revenues and bring finally our budget into balance.[17]

After the World War II ended, income tax rates were reduced to 3 percent which helped the economy to grow and tax revenues to increase. Reflecting on this, Kennedy stated November 20, 1962:

> The soundest way to raise the revenues in the long run is to cut the rates now. The experience of a number of European countries and Japan have borne this out.
>
> This country's own experience with tax reduction in 1954 has borne this out...
>
> And the reason is that only full employment can balance the budget, and tax reduction can pave the way to that employment.[46]

On January 24, 1963, Kennedy stated:

> The largest single barrier to full employment of our manpower and resources and to a higher rate of economic growth is the unrealistically heavy drag of Federal income taxes on private purchasing power, initiative and incentive.[47]

John F. Kennedy stated February 2, 1961:

> Expansion and modernization of the nation's productive plant is essential to accelerate economic growth and to improve the international competitive position of American industry...
>
> An early stimulus to business investment will promote recovery and increase employment.[48]

Kennedy told the National Industrial Conference Board, February 13, 1961:

> We must start now to provide additional stimulus to the modernization of American industrial plants...
>
> I shall propose to the Congress a new tax incentive for businesses to expand their normal investment in plant and equipment.[49]

Kennedy described this in his report on the State of the National Economy, August 13, 1962:

> A bill will be presented to the Congress for action next year. It will include an across the board, top to bottom cut in both corporate and personal income taxes.
>
> It will include long-needed tax reform that logic and equity demand...
>
> The billions of dollars this bill will place in the hands of the consumer and our businessmen will have both immediate and permanent benefits to our economy. Every dollar released from taxation that is spent or invested will help create a new job and a new salary.

And these new jobs and new salaries can create other jobs and other salaries and more customers and more growth for an expanding American economy.[51]

Kennedy wrote November 20, 1962:

This administration pledged itself last summer to an across-the-board, top-to-bottom cut in personal and corporate income taxes...

Next year's tax bill should reduce personal as well as corporate income taxes, for those in the lower brackets, who are certain to spend their additional take-home pay, and for those in the middle and upper brackets, who can thereby be encouraged to undertake additional efforts and enabled to invest more capital...

I am confident that the enactment of the right bill next year will in due course increase our gross national product by several times the amount of taxes actually cut.[52]

KEYNES' STIMULUS PLAN - GO IN DEBT

When the Korean War started in 1951, Americans again accepted a rise in income taxes during wartime.

Another issue was inflation. Inflation occurs when too many dollars are chasing too few goods, causing prices to rise.

Economist John Maynard Keynes introduced the theory of using a graduated income tax to prevent inflation by intentionally removing dollars from the money supply.

Graduated income tax rates started at 11 percent.

Keynes also gave the questionable legacy of 'debt-stimulated economy' - recommending the government to go in debt - to spend money in the private sector to create jobs - which would increase national production and bring in tax revenue - which would pay off the government debt.

To put this in perspective, if a small business owner needed a piece of equipment to expand his business, he had two choices:

1) Work harder, save up money, spend less on other items, and purchase the equipment;

or

2) Charge it on a credit card, use the equipment to increase business, then use the profits to pay off the credit card.

Unfortunately, Congress fell into the habit of never paying off the credit card. They routinely increased the debt, hoping the next the Congress would be more responsible and pay it off.

Representatives yielded to the temptation of increasing the debt in order to funnel money into pork projects, entitlement constituencies and corporate favoritism hoping to buy votes for their next election.

Keynes 'debt-stimulated economy' has left America with a multi-trillion dollar debt where nearly all tax revenue is used just to pay the interest on the debt.

DEBT & DECLINE

Debt was a contributing factor in the decline of many great nations, including the:

Han Dynasty of China,
Roman Empire,
Byzantine Empire;
Kublai Khan's Yuan Dynasty;
Spanish Hapsburg Dynasty;
Ottoman Empire;
French Empire,
Britain's United Kingdom, and
the Soviet Union.

Niall Ferguson, a *Newsweek* columnist and the Laurence A. Tisch Professor of History at Harvard University, wrote in 'How Economic Weakness Endangers the U.S.' (3/13/10):

> If the United States succumbs to a fiscal crisis, as an increasing number of economic experts fear it may, then the entire balance of global economic power could shift...
> Call the United States what you like - superpower, hegemon, or empire - but its ability to manage its finances is closely tied to its ability to remain the predominant global military power...
> The disciples of John Maynard Keynes argue that increasing the federal debt by roughly a third was necessary to avoid Depression 2.0...
> That's a bigger deficit than any seen in

the past 60 years — only slightly larger in relative terms than the deficit in 1942. We are, it seems, having the fiscal policy of a world war, without the war...

There is no end in sight to the borrowing binge. Unless entitlements are cut or taxes are raised, there will never be another balanced budget...

Calculate the net present value of the unfunded liabilities of the Social Security and Medicare systems. One recent estimate puts them at about $104 trillion, 10 times the stated federal debt.

No sweat, reply the Keynesians. We can easily finance $1 trillion a year of new government debt... Unfortunately for this argument, the evidence to support it is lacking...

According to Fred Bergsten of the Peterson Institute for International Economics, if this trend were to continue, the U.S. -current-account deficit could rise to 15 percent of GDP by 2030, and its net debt to the rest of the world could hit 140 percent of GDP...

Now, who said the following?

"My prediction is that politicians will eventually be tempted to resolve the (fiscal) crisis the way irresponsible governments usually do: by printing money, both to pay current bills and to inflate away debt. And as that temptation becomes obvious, interest rates will soar."

The surprising thing is that this was none other than Paul Krugman, the high priest of Keynesianism...

The history of all the great European empires is replete with such episodes. Indeed, serial default and high inflation have tended to be the surest symptoms of imperial decline...

History suggests that once you are spending as much as a fifth of your revenues on debt service, you have a problem...

This is how empires decline. It begins with a debt explosion. It ends with an inexorable reduction in the resources available for the Army, Navy, and Air Force.

Which is why voters are right to worry about America's debt crisis...

If the United States doesn't come up soon with a credible plan to restore the federal budget to balance over the next five to 10 years, the danger is very real that a debt crisis could lead to a major weakening of American power...

The precedents are certainly there.

Habsburg Spain defaulted on all or part of its debt 14 times between 1557 and 1696 and also succumbed to inflation due to a surfeit of New World silver.

Pre-revolutionary France was spending 62 percent of royal revenue on debt service by 1788.

The Ottoman Empire went the same way: interest payments and amortization rose from 15 percent of the budget in 1860 to 50 percent in 1875.

And don't forget the last great English-speaking empire. By the interwar years, interest payments were consuming 44 percent of the British budget, making it intensely difficult to rearm in the face of a new German threat.

Call it the fatal arithmetic of imperial decline. Without radical fiscal reform, it could apply to America next.

Mercy Otis Warren referred to Spain's economic strain. She was the wife of James Warren, president of the Massachusetts Provincial Congress, and brother of James Otis, who argued against British 'writs of assistance' where tax collectors searched and confiscated private property.

Mercy Otis Warren was called 'The Conscience of the Revolution' as she corresponded with Samuel Adams, John Hancock, Patrick Henry, Thomas Jefferson, George Washington, Martha Washington, John Adams, Abigail Adams, and Hannah Winthrop, admonishing them to contend for freedom.

Warning that America's 'Federal City' might collect taxes like Spain's capital of Madrid, Mercy Otis Warren wrote in *Observations on the New Constitution, and on the Federal and State Conventions*, 1788:

> When the inhabitants of the Eastern States are dragging out a miserable existence, only on the gleanings of their fields; and the Southern, blessed with a softer and more fertile climate, are languishing in hopeless poverty; and when asked, what is become of the flower of their crop, and the rich produce of their farms - they may answer in the hapless style of the Man of La Mancha,
>
> 'The steward of my Lord has seized and sent it to Madrid.'
>
> Or, in the more literal language of truth, The exigencies of government require that the collectors of the revenue should transmit it to the Federal City.

Benjamin Franklin mentioned Spain squandering its riches in *The Way to Wealth*, 1758:

> If you would be wealthy, says he...think of saving as well as of getting:
> the Indies have not made Spain rich, because her outgoes are greater than her incomes.

Franklin expounded further of the dangers of debt in *The Way to Wealth*, 1758:

> God gives all things to industry. Then plough deep, while sluggards sleep, and you shall have corn to sell and to keep, says Poor Dick.
> Work while it is called today, for you know not how much you may be hindered tomorrow, which makes Poor Richard say, one today is worth two tomorrows; and farther, have you somewhat to do tomorrow, do it today...
> And in another place, pride breakfasted with plenty, dined with poverty, and supped with infamy...
> What madness must it be to run in debt for these superfluities! We are offered, by the terms of this vendue, six months' credit; and that perhaps has induced some of us to attend it, because we cannot spare the ready money, and hope now to be fine without it.
> But, ah, think what you do when you run in debt; you give to another power over your liberty...
> If you cannot pay at the time, you will be ashamed to see your creditor; you will be in fear when you speak to him, you will make poor pitiful sneaking excuses, and by degrees come to lose

you veracity, and sink into base downright lying; for, as Poor Richard says, the second vice is lying, the first is running in debt. And again to the same purpose, lying rides upon debt's back...

Poverty often deprives a man of all spirit and virtue: 'tis hard for an empty bag to stand upright, as Poor Richard truly says...

And yet you are about to put yourself under that tyranny when you run in debt for such dress! Your creditor has authority at his pleasure to deprive you of your liberty, by confining you in gaol (jail) for life, or to sell you for a servant, if you should not be able to pay him!

When you have got your bargain, you may, perhaps, think little of payment; but creditors, Poor Richard tells us, have better memories than debtors...

The day comes round before you are aware, and the demand is made before you are prepared to satisfy it... Time will seem to have added wings to his heels as well as shoulders. Those have a short Lent, saith Poor Richard, who owe money to be paid at Easter.

Then since, as he says, the borrower is a slave to the lender, and the debtor to the creditor, disdain the chain, preserve your freedom; and maintain your independency: be industrious and free; be frugal and free.

At present, perhaps, you may think yourself in thriving circumstances, and that you can bear a little extravagance without injury; but,
For age and want, save while you may;
No morning sun lasts a whole day,
as Poor Richard says.

Gain may be temporary and uncertain, but ever while you live, expense is constant and certain...as Poor Richard says. So rather go to bed supperless than rise in debt.

W illiam R. Hawkins is Senior Fellow for National Security Studies at the U.S. Business and Industry Council. He was formerly an economics professor at Appalachian State University, the University of North Carolina-Asheville, and Radford University.

William R. Hawkins wrote in his article 'Spanish Lessons' (AmericanEconomicAlert.org, April 7, 2004):

It may be hard for most people to imagine, but Spain was the first global Superpower.

It gained this status as the defender of Europe against Muslim armies and by leading the West's exploration of America.

In 1492, the same year that Spanish-financed Christopher Columbus discovered the New World, the last Muslim stronghold of Granada was ceded to Ferdinand and Isabella to complete the Catholic Reconquest of the Iberian Peninsula.

With Spain as its political base, and gold and silver flowing in from its American colonies, the Hapsburg dynasty became the dominant power in Europe.

It controlled rich parts of Italy through Naples and Milan, and Central Europe from the Netherlands through the Holy Roman Empire to Austria.

In the 16th century it added the far distant Philippine islands to its empire.

The Hapsburgs held off the Ottoman Turks, whose resurgent wave of Islamic conquest in the 16th century swept across the Balkans and nearly captured Vienna.

The Hapsburgs went into decline in the 17th century, and while any such momentous event has many causes, for our purposes the focus will be on the economic collapse of Spain...

The demands of empire required a strong and growing economy, but Spain did not keep up with the economic expansion that was taking place in other parts of Europe.

Madrid's financial base fell out from under its empire.

Spain could continue to consume in the short term because of the flow of precious metals from American mines, but it could not produce the goods it needed at home, which in the long-run proved fatal to its standing as a Great Power...

Spanish imports were double exports and the precious metals became scarce within weeks of the arrival of the American treasure fleets as the money flowed to Spain's many creditors...

Spanish leaders were deluded by a sense of false prosperity.

This is testified by the statement of a prominent official, Alfonso Nunez de Castro in 1675:

'Let London manufacture those fine fabrics of hers to her heart's content; let Holland her chambrays; Florence her cloth; the Indies their beaver and vicuna; Milan her brocade, Italy and Flanders their linens... so long as our capital can enjoy them; the only thing it proves is that all nations train their journeymen for Madrid, and that Madrid is the queen of Parliaments, for all the world serves her and she serves nobody.'

A few years later, the Madrid government was bankrupt.

The Spanish nobleman had foolishly elevated consumption, a use for wealth, above production, the creation of wealth...

Spain's rivals, France, Holland (which started a successful revolt in 1568) and England, prospered by their trade surpluses, and reinvested the money to expand their own capabilities...

Rival powers were able to field and finance military forces that could defeat the once superior Spanish forces both on land and at sea.

The irony of this is that Spain was ruled by a warrior aristocracy tempered by centuries of constant warfare against Islamic hordes and Christian heretics.

These nobles looked down on merchants and manufacturers and disparaged their mundane professions only to find that without a strong domestic business class they could not afford the fleets and armies that guarded the empire they had built.

Today, the American 'empire' is also trying to consume more than it produces. The U.S. trade deficit is nearing Spain's nadir of imports being double exports.

Both government spending and private consumption are financed heavily by debt.

Washington is printing money, the modern equivalent of digging gold out of the ground, rather than earning the means to pay its bills.

And the political and military elites are apparently indifferent to the fate of domestic business and industry.

Americans must learn more from the

Spanish experience than just the perils of
appeasing terrorists — and take corrective action
while they still can.

৵

Don Keko wrote in 'Debt and the Collapse of
Civilizations' (Sept. 11, 2010, www.examiner.com)

The American government has been
overspending for a decade... that spending has
kicked into overdrive...

Civilizations that overspend without
modifying their habits collapse.

Overspending has destroyed some of
history's greatest civilizations and
empires including Han China, the Roman Empire,
the French Empire, and the Soviet Union.

The Han were one of China's greatest
dynasties. The dynasty ruled for about four
centuries from 206 B.C. to 220 A.D.

Han rule is considered a golden age and
their influence extends to the modern day. The
majority ethnic group in modern China consider
themselves 'Han.'

The empire enjoyed a thriving economy
that reached Rome and India.

The government spent on infrastructure
improvements, tried to provide poor relief, and
allowed merchants to engage in money making
ventures.

As time wore on, the government
required more funds for their projects.

Additionally, they wanted to control the
largely autonomous large landowners.

In response to the need for cash and desire to control the upper classes, the government increased regulations, taxes, and spending.

The Han even began nationalizing industries. Government actions crushed the merchants, led to deficit spending, and weakened the economy.

Government debt increased dramatically weakening stability...

The government could no longer respond to threats inside and outside of China...and eventually collapsed under the weight of its economic policies.

Han China's fall resembles that of the Roman Empire's.

The Romans built the greatest empire in history.

The empire prospered from its founding in 31 B.C. until the third century. During the third century, the economy and political structure collapsed.

Hyperinflation, currency devaluation, and overspending doomed the empire.

Roman trade networks completely collapsed.

Imperial contenders fought each other and spent personal and government money on soldiers.

Eventually, the political situation settled, but the economy never recovered.

Diocletian ended the political turmoil in 284 A.D. and tried to restore the economy.

His political solution lasted until 312 A.D. and his economic reforms never worked.

Emperors struggled to maintain control throughout the fourth century.

They spent tremendous resources on the military to defend themselves against upstarts and barbarian invaders.

Taxes increased dramatically.

People refused to work and the army requisitioned taxes in the form of foodstuffs.

The empire could not afford the men to defend the borders.

Eventually, the weight of spending crushed the empire and it collapsed in 476 A.D. Roman emperors taxed their citizens as far as they could.

The French kings taxed their citizens even further. The French court spent lavishly on themselves.

Instead of building infrastructure and cultivating a climate friendly to economic development, they built palaces, fought several wars against Britain, and taxed their citizens in every conceivable way.

The government even forced people to do manual labor as a form of taxation.

The French people suffered under the oppressive taxation.

They also suffered from famine and malnutrition as a result of the Little Ice Age.

As people starved and struggled to pay their taxes, the nobles lived unbelievably lavish lives.

The government continued to spend freely. France teetered on the edge of economic collapse.

When Louis XVI agreed to help finance the American Revolution, France went bankrupt... National debt collapsed the system.

Louis was forced to take drastic action.

Events spiraled out of his control and the monarchy collapsed.

The economic crisis that precipitated the French Revolution led to 26 years of bloodshed and instability in Europe.

Like Revolutionary France, the Soviet Union collapsed under the weight of debt.

Throughout the Cold War period, the Soviets and United States engaged in an arms race and waged proxy wars across the world.

By the late seventies, the Soviets appeared on the verge of victory in the Cold War.

However, the invasion of Afghanistan and election of Ronald Reagan changed the dynamic and forced Soviet spending to unprecedented levels.

The Soviet economy spent billions fighting in Afghanistan. It became an economic and military black hole. The Soviets struggled to fight the American backed Afghan rebels.

At the same time, President Reagan began an unprecedented peacetime military buildup. The Soviets felt compelled to try to keep up. The more dynamic American economy boomed while the Soviet economy sputtered.

By 1989, the Soviets could no longer afford to keep their empire.

They allowed the East European satellite nations to leave. In 1991, the U.S.S.R. itself collapsed under the weight of its debt.

Rolf Nef is an independent asset manager in Zurich, Switzerland. He is a Graduate from the University of Zurich in economics, with more than 25 years of experience in financial markets. He manages 'Tell Gold & Silber Fonds', a regulated hedge-fund according to Liechtenstein law.

Rolf Nef wrote in 'Falling Empires and their Currencies' (Part I: From the Fall of Rome to the Fall of the British Empire, Global Research, Jan. 15, 2007):

> When empires fall, their currencies fall first. Even clearer is the rising debt of empires in decline, because in most cases their physical expansion is financed with debt...
>
> The common thing is that the currencies of each and every one of these falling empires lost dramatically in value...
>
> The silver content of Roman coins... The Roman Empire existed from 400 B.C. to 400 A.D.
>
> Its history is the history of physical expansion, like the history of almost all empires. Its expansion was driven by a citizen soldier army, paid in silver coins, land and slaves from occupied territories.
>
> If there was not enough silver in the treasury to conduct a war, base metals were added to coin more money. That is to say, the authorities debased their currency which presaged the fall of the Empire.
>
> There was a limit to the expansion. The empire became over-stretched, running out of silver money, and eventually went under, overrun by barbarian hordes...
>
> The second case is France during the time of the Bourbon monarchs who ruled France from 1589 to their fall in the French Revolution in 1792...

The kings of France were constantly fighting overseas wars in Africa and America, and, of course, financed those wars with credit.

The so-called Seven Years' War (1756-1763) proved to be very expensive for France.

The outcome of that war, in a bitter fight with Britain over their American colonies, was that France lost almost all significant foothold in the Americas and its navy fleet as well.

Britain emerged as the dominant power in the world. The land of the colonies, and its potential tax revenues to the French state, were gone, but the debt and the cost of interest remained.

In 1781, the cost of interest as a percentage of tax income was 24 percent.

By 1790 it had risen to a staggering 95 percent of total tax revenue!

Tax was paid only by the so-called Third Estate–peasants, working people and the bourgeoisie, i.e. the mass of the population– but not by the Church or the nobility.

Not surprisingly, the French Revolution started.

The nobility was hanged on the lantern posts of Paris, the church lost all its property, and the king got beheaded at the guillotine...

The British only looked like the winners, but the Napoleonic wars from 1805 to Waterloo in 1815, and the loss of the American colonies (these ruthless guys didn't want to pay taxes to king George to finance his wars for conquering and looting other peoples and lands), drove His Majesty's government debt to the sky...

But the better way of financing it with the perpetual consols and annuities with the Bank of

England (which was founded in 1694 by King William III and his business friends from Amsterdam on a private basis), saved them from bankruptcy.

Nevertheless, the Bank of England had to stop the exchange from paper to gold.

Their great good fortune was that the industrial revolution with the steam engine started in England, which brought unprecedented economic growth and let the debt fall in relative terms...

France after Waterloo had been militarily beaten and no other enemy or rival for global hegemony was in sight.

The 19th century was the time when the British upper class had the time to spend all the loot and plunder from its colonies.

They came to Switzerland, climbed the mountains (Matterhorn was first climbed by a British climber).

They were the first to go to St. Moritz in wintertime holidays, as well as many other places.

They were perceived as gentleman, because here so much money could only be earned by hard and serious work, at least at that time.

But France and generally the Continent remained the potential enemy.

When Bismarck started war against France in 1871, London found it to its liking, as it was to her advantage to have a weakened France.

But the defeat of France gave birth not only to a new united Germany under Bismark and Prussia, but also to a new economic powerhouse, Germany.

Britain, where the first Kondratieff cycle

(high economic growth followed by low growth) started with the steam engine fell into a heavy depression by 1873.

But Germany started the new Kondratieff cycle with the diesel-, gasoline- and electric engine (founders were all German: Messers. Diesel, Otto and Siemens).

Soon Germany was producing more steel than England.

The new source of energy, oil, made the German war ships faster than the English one, something of great concern to London.

When Deutsche Bank and Georg von Siemens initiated the Baghdad railway, which went from Berlin through the Austrian empire, Serbia and into the Ottoman Empire to the oil fields in Kirkuk, north of Baghdad (oil was at that time only known in Baku, Russia, Kirkuk and Pennsylvania, USA).

The new German rail link with Baghdad was out of range of British sea power and their controlled waterways. The alarm bells went on in Whitehall (Palace of English Monarchs).

When a young new German Kaiser, Wilhelm II became Kaiser in 1888, he began to assert his own role in foreign policy in direct challenge to the system of the Iron Chancellor, Bismark, who had carefully forged a system of alliances around Germany to ensure her peace and economic freedom.

In 1890 Bismarck, got sacked by Kaiser Willhelm, because Wilhelm wanted colonies and Empire like his relatives who were monarchs in England, France and Spain.

With Bismark gone, the British decided for a war, one in which the Continental powers would crucify each other.

Britain calculated she could easily break up the tottering Ottoman Empire in order to get Mesopotamia with Kirkuk and its oil under control, to pull the plug on the emerging German oil line to Baghdad and to take Mesopotamia and the oil-rich Middle East including Persia itself. The plan is what became known in history as World War I.

It didn't quite turn out as hoped by London. Instead of being a war lasting a few weeks as had been expected, the undertaking was huge and costly, lasted over four years, cost millions of lives and was fought on a global theatre...

The Prince of Austria, Francis Ferdinand, heir to the Austro-Hungarian Empire, got shot in Sarajewo. That event started the war with the declaration of Austria against Serbia, which in turn drove Russia against Austria and kick-started all the tangled web of mutual defense treaties across Europe.

By August 1914, Russia, Austria, Germany, France and UK were all at war.

In 1917 a British army marched into Baghdad...and got the oilfields under control.

The Ottoman Empire fell and the continental European powers crucified each other.

The British got what they wanted, but at huge cost. The government debt rose from 20 percent of GNP in 1914 to 190 percent in 1920...

The reparation demands by the victors against Germany...of course Germany could not pay... It laid the basis for the next World War II.

CONCLUSION

The three motivations for taxation were to

1) pay for legitimate government expenditures,
2) economic engineering and
3) social engineering.

Taxes expanded from Tariff and Excise Taxes to include Income Taxes, especially during war time.

Churches did social work, helped produced a moral populace which kept crime low, were exempt from income taxes, and spoke out on politics.

When Woodrow Wilson instituted the Income Tax, wealthy industrialists wanted to avoid these taxes so they joined the church tax exempt category by forming educational and charitable foundations.

Communist leaning groups form tax exempt organizations, resulting in Congress limiting political involvement of tax exempt organizations.

Lyndon B. Johnson wanted to silence tax exempt organizations who were accusing him of being communist-leaning.

Franklin Roosevelt's tax increase during World War II increased outsourcing.

Squeeze the sponge and the water flows out. Investment and jobs flowed to other countries as a result of the anti-business squeeze of:
-Higher Taxes;
-Higher Wages & Benefits;
-More Lawsuits;
-Increased Government Bureaucracy

-Environmental Protection Agency
restrictions; and
-'Crony Capitalism' where companies
supporting the politicians in power received
favoritism and those not supporting them did
not.

Kennedy's stimulus plan was to reduce taxes.
John Maynard Keynes' stimulus plan was to go in debt.

Like charging up more credit cards, Keynes' plan made the situation worse, as Congress was tempted to increase debt to fund projects and programs to benefit their re-elections.

To turn things around, there needs to be a political will to make it more profitable for businesses to be located in American than overseas.

Growing concern exists with the admission of the IRS targeting groups holding political views different than the President's, the head of the IRS pleading the 5th Amendment rather than answering questions at a Congressional hearing, and with the IRS being put in charge of the national healthcare plan.

Whatever tax plan is eventually adopted in America, the security of our Nation will never be in 'a plan.'

There will always be the need for 'eternal vigilance' by the citizens.

Noah Webster stated in his *History of the United States*, 1832:

If the citizens neglect their duty and place unprincipled men in office, the government will soon be corrupted; laws will be made not for the public good so much as for the selfish or local purposes;

Corrupt or incompetent men will be appointed to execute the laws; the public revenues will be squandered on unworthy men; and the rights of the citizens will be violated or disregarded...

If a republican government fails to secure public prosperity and happiness, it must be because the citizens neglect the divine commands, and elect bad men to make and administer the laws.[54]

In 1988, President Ronald Reagan stated:

I believe we really can, however, say that God did give mankind virtually unlimited gifts to invent, produce and create. And for that reason alone, it would be wrong for governments to devise a tax structure that suppresses and denies those gifts.[55]

Maybe someday, if Americans act responsibly, April 15th will be remembered for something positive, instead of the date Abraham Lincoln died in 1865, or the date the Titanic sank in 1912, or the date income taxes are due.

APPENDIX

Davy Crockett served 3 terms in the U.S. Congress from 1827-31 and 1833-35. He died in the Battle of the Alamo, Texas. *The Life of Colonel David Crockett* by Edward Sylvester Ellis (1884) relates the story of Davy Crockett's congressional speech, "Not Yours to Give." In the House of Representatives a bill was taken up appropriating money for the benefit of a widow of a distinguished naval officer. Several beautiful speeches had been made in its support. The speaker was just about to put the question when Crockett arose:

"Mr. Speaker-I have as much respect for the memory of the deceased, and as much sympathy for the suffering of the living, if there be, as any man in this House, but we must not permit our respect for the dead or our sympathy for part of the living to lead us into an act of injustice to the balance of the living.

I will not go into an argument to prove that Congress has not the power to appropriate this money as an act of charity. Every member on this floor knows it. We have the right as individuals, to give away as much of our own money as we please in charity; but as members of Congress we have no right to appropriate a dollar of the public money. Some eloquent appeals have been made to us upon the ground that it is a debt due the deceased.

Mr. Speaker, the deceased lived long after the close of the war; he was in office to the day of his death, and I ever heard that the government was in arrears to him. Every man in this House knows it is not a debt. We cannot without the grossest corruption, appropriate this money as the payment of a debt. We have not the semblance of authority to appropriate it as charity.

Mr. Speaker, I have said we have the right to give as much money of our own as we please. I am the poorest man on this floor. I cannot vote for this bill, but I will give one week's pay to the object, and if every member of Congress will do the same, it will amount to more than the bill asks."

He took his seat. Nobody replied. The bill was put upon its passage, and, instead of passing unanimously, as was generally supposed, and as, no doubt, it would, but for that speech, it received but few votes, and, of course, was lost.

Later, when asked by a friend why he had opposed the appropriation, Crockett gave this explanation:

"Several years ago I was one evening standing on the steps of the Capitol with some members of Congress, when our attention was attracted by a great light over in Georgetown. It was evidently a large fire.

"We jumped into a hack and drove over as fast as we could. In spite of all that could be done, many houses were burned and many families made houseless, and besides, some of them had lost all but the clothes they had on. The weather was very cold, and when I saw so many children suffering, I felt that something ought to be done for them.

"The next morning a bill was introduced appropriating $20,000 for their relief. We put aside all other business and rushed it through as soon as it could be done. The next summer, when it began to be time to think about election, I concluded I would take a scout around among the boys of my district. I had no opposition there but, as the election was some time off, I did not know what might turn up.

"When riding one day in a part of my district in which I was more of a stranger than any other, I saw a man in a field plowing and coming toward the road. I gauged my gait so that we should meet as he came up, I spoke to the man. He replied politely, but as I thought, rather coldly. I began:

'Well friend, I am one of those unfortunate beings called candidates and-

'Yes I know you; you are Colonel Crockett. I have seen you once before, and voted for you the last time you were elected. I suppose you are out electioneering now, but you had better not waste your time or mine, I shall not vote for you again.'

This was a sockdolger? I begged him tell me what was the matter.

'Well Colonel, it is hardly worthwhile to waste time or words upon it. I do not see how it can be mended, but you gave a vote last winter which shows that either you have not capacity to understand the Constitution, or that you are wanting in the honesty and firmness to be guided by it. In either case you are not the man to represent me.

'But I beg your pardon for expressing it that way. I did not intend to avail myself of the privilege of the constituent to speak plainly to a candidate for the purpose of insulting you or wounding you.

'I intend by it only to say that your understanding of the constitution is very different from mine; and I will say to you what but for my rudeness, I should not have said, that I believe you to be honest. But an understanding of the constitution different from mine I cannot overlook, because the Constitution, to be worth anything, must be held sacred, and rigidly observed in all its provisions.

'The man who wields power and misinterprets it is the more dangerous the honest he is. I admit the truth of all you say, but there must be some mistake. Though I live in the backwoods and seldom go from home, I take the papers from Washington and read very carefully all the proceedings of Congress. My papers say you voted for a bill to appropriate $20,000 to some sufferers by fire in Georgetown. Is that true?'

'Well my friend; I may as well own up. You have got me there. But certainly nobody will complain that a great and rich country like ours should give the insignificant sum of $20,000 to relieve its suffering women and children, particularly with a full and overflowing treasury, and I am sure, if you had been there, you would have done just the same as I did.'

'It is not the amount, Colonel, that I complain of; it is the principle. In the first place, the government ought to have in the Treasury no more than enough for its legitimate purposes. But that has nothing with the question. The power of collecting and disbursing money at pleasure is the most dangerous power that can be entrusted to man, particularly under our system of collecting revenue by a tariff, which reaches every man in the country, no matter how poor he may be, and the poorer he is the more he pays in proportion to his means.

'What is worse, it presses upon him without his knowledge

where the weight centers, for there is not a man in the United States who can ever guess how much he pays to the government. So you see, that while you are contributing to relieve one, you are drawing it from thousands who are even worse off than he. If you had the right to give anything, the amount was simply a matter of discretion with you, and you had as much right to give $20,000,000 as $20,000. If you have the right to give at all; and as the Constitution neither defines charity nor stipulates the amount, you are at liberty to give to any and everything which you may believe, or profess to believe, is a charity and to any amount you may think proper. You will very easily perceive what a wide door this would open for fraud and corruption and favoritism, on the one hand, and for robbing the people on the other.

'No, Colonel, Congress has no right to give charity. Individual members may give as much of their own money as they please, but they have no right to touch a dollar of the public money for that purpose. If twice as many houses had been burned in this country as in Georgetown, neither you nor any other member of Congress would have thought of appropriating a dollar for our relief. There are about two hundred and forty members of Congress.

'If they had shown their sympathy for the sufferers by contributing each one week's pay, it would have made over $13,000. There are plenty of wealthy men around Washington who could have given $20,000 without depriving themselves of even a luxury of life. The congressmen chose to keep their own money, which, if reports be true, some of them spend not very creditably; and the people about Washington, no doubt, applauded you for relieving them from necessity of giving what was not yours to give. The people have delegated to Congress, by the Constitution, the power to do certain things.

'To do these, it is authorized to collect and pay moneys, and for nothing else. Everything beyond this is usurpation, and a violation of the Constitution. So you see, Colonel, you have violated the Constitution in what I consider a vital point. It is a precedent fraught with danger to the country, for when Congress once begins to stretch its power beyond the limits of the Constitution, there is no limit to it, and no security for the people. I have no doubt you acted honestly, but that does not make it any better, except as far as you are personally concerned, and you see that I cannot vote for you.'

I tell you I felt streaked. I saw if I should have opposition, and this man should go to talking and in that district I was a gone fawnskin. I could not answer him, and the fact is, I was so fully convinced that he was right, I did not want to. But I must satisfy him, and I said to him:

'Well, my friend, you hit the nail upon the head when you said I had not sense enough to understand the Constitution. I intended to be guided by it, and thought I had studied it fully. I have heard many speeches in Congress about the powers of Congress, but what you have said here at your plow has got more hard, sound sense in it than all the fine speeches I ever heard. If I had ever taken the view of it that you have, I would have put my head into the fire before I would have given that vote; and if you will forgive me and vote for me again, if I ever vote for another unconstitutional law I wish I may be shot.'

He laughingly replied;

'Yes, Colonel, you have sworn to that once before, but I will trust you again upon one condition. You are convinced that your vote was wrong. Your acknowledgment of it will do more good than beating you for it. If, as you go around the district, you will tell people about this vote, and that you are satisfied it was wrong, I will not only vote for you, but will do what I can to keep down opposition, and perhaps, I may exert some little influence in that way.'

'If I don't,' said I, 'I wish I may be shot; and to convince you that I am in earnest in what I say I will come back this way in a week or ten days, and if you will get up a gathering of people, I will make a speech to them. Get up a barbecue, and I will pay for it.'

'No, Colonel, we are not rich people in this section but we have plenty of provisions to contribute for a barbecue, and some to spare for those who have none. The push of crops will be over in a few days, and we can then afford a day for a barbecue. This Thursday; I will see to getting it up on Saturday week. Come to my house on Friday, and we will go together, and I promise you a very respectable crowd to see and hear you.'

'Well I will be here. But one thing more before I say goodbye. I must know your name.'

'My name is Bunce.'

'Not Horatio Bunce?'

'Yes'

'Well, Mr. Bunce, I never saw you before, though you say you have seen me, but I know you very well. I am glad I have met you, and very proud that I may hope to have you for my friend.'

It was one of the luckiest hits of my life that I met him. He mingled but little with the public, but was widely known for his remarkable intelligence, and for a heart brim-full and running over with kindness and benevolence, which showed themselves not only in words but in acts. He was the oracle of the whole country around him, and his fame had extended far beyond the circle of his immediate acquaintance. Though I had never met him, before, I had heard much of him, and but for this meeting it is very likely I should have had opposition, and had been beaten. One thing is very certain, no man could now stand up in that district under such a vote.

At the appointed time I was at his house, having told our conversation to every crowd I had met, and to every man I stayed all night with, and I found that it gave the people an interest and confidence in me stronger than I had ever seen manifested before. Though I was considerably fatigued when I reached his house, and, under ordinary circumstances, should have gone early to bed, I kept him up until midnight talking about the principles and affairs of government, and got more real, true knowledge of them than I had got all my life before.

I have known and seen much of him since, for I respect him - no, that is not the word - I reverence and love him more than any living man, and I go to see him two or three times every year; and I will tell you, sir, if every one who professes to be a Christian lived and acted and enjoyed it as he does, the religion of Christ would take the world by storm. But to return to my story.

The next morning we went to the barbecue and, to my surprise, found about a thousand men there. I met a good many whom I had not known before, and they and my friend introduced me around until I had got pretty well acquainted - at least, they all knew me. In due time notice was given that I would speak to them. They gathered up around a stand that had been erected. I opened my speech by saying:

'Fellow-citizens - I present myself before you today feeling like a new man. My eyes have lately been opened to truths which ignorance or prejudice or both, had heretofore hidden from my view. I feel that I can today offer you the ability to render you more valuable service than I have ever been able to render before. I am here today more for the purpose of acknowledging my error than to seek your votes. That I should make this acknowledgment is due to myself as well as to you. Whether you will vote for me is a matter for your consideration only.'

I went on to tell them about the fire and my vote for the appropriation and then told them why I was satisfied it was wrong. I closed by saying:

'And now, fellow-citizens, it remains only for me to tell you that the most of the speech you have listened to with so much interest was simply a repetition of the arguments by which your neighbor, Mr. Bunce, convinced me of my error. It is the best speech I ever made in my life, but he is entitled to the credit for it. And now I hope he is satisfied with his convert and that he will get up here and tell you so.'

He came up to the stand and said:

'Fellow-citizens - it affords me great pleasure to comply with the request of Colonel Crockett. I have always considered him a thoroughly honest man, and I am satisfied that he will faithfully perform all that he has promised you today.'

He went down, and there went up from that crowd such a shout for Davy Crockett as his name never called forth before. I am not much given to tears, but I was taken with a choking then and felt some big drops rolling down my cheeks. And I tell you now that the remembrance of those few words spoken by such a man, and the honest, hearty shout they produced, is worth more to me than all the honors I have received and all the reputation I have ever made, or ever shall make, as a member of Congress.

Now, sir, concluded Crockett, you know why I made that speech yesterday. There is one thing which I will call your attention, you remember that I proposed to give a week's pay. There are in that House many very wealthy men - men who think nothing of spending a week's pay, or a dozen of them, for a dinner or a wine party when they have something to accomplish by it.

Some of those same men made beautiful speeches upon the great debt of gratitude which the country owed the deceased-a debt which could not be paid by money-and the insignificance and worthlessness of money, particularly so insignificant a sum as $20,000 when weighed against the honor of the nation. Yet not one of them responded to my proposition. Money with them is nothing but trash when it is to come out of the people. But it is the one great thing for which most of them are striving, and many of them sacrifice honor, integrity, and justice to obtain it."

APPENDIX

Andrew Jackson stated in his 8th Annual Message, December 5, 1836:

Our gratitude is due to the Supreme Ruler of the Universe, and I invite you to unite with me in offering to Him fervent supplications that His providential care may ever be extended to those who follow us, enabling them to avoid the dangers and the horrors of war consistently with a just and indispensable regard to the rights and honor of our country....

The experience of other nations admonished us to hasten the extinguishment of the public debt.... No political maxim is better established than that which tells us that an improvident expenditure of money is the parent of profligacy, and that no people can hope to perpetuate their liberties who long acquiesce in a policy which taxes them for objects not necessary to the legitimate and real wants of their Government....

The shortest reflection must satisfy everyone that to require the people to pay taxes to the Government merely that they may be paid back again is sporting with the substantial interests of the country, and no system which produces such a result can be expected to receive the public countenance.

Nothing could be gained by it even if each individual who contributed a portion of the tax could receive back promptly the same portion.... The practical effect of such an attempt must ever be to burden the people with taxes, not for the purposes beneficial to them, but to swell the profits of deposit banks and support a band of useless public officers.

A distribution to the people is impracticable and unjust in other respects. It would be taking one man's property and giving it to another. Such would be the unavoidable result of a rule of equality....

We know that they contribute unequally, and a rule, therefore, that would distribute to them equally would be liable to all the objections which apply to the principle of an equal division of property. To make the General Government the instrument of carrying this odious principle into effect would be at once to destroy the means of its usefulness and change the character designed for it by the framers of the Constitution....

The Government had without necessity received from the people a large surplus....The banks proceeded to make loans upon this surplus, and thus converted it into banking capital, and in this manner it has tended to multiply bank charters and has had a great agency in producing a spirit of wild speculation.

The possession and use of the property out of which this surplus was created belonged to the people, but the Government has transferred its possession to incorporated banks, whose interest and effort it is to make large profits out of its use....

Congress is only authorized to levy taxes "to pay the debts and provide for the common defense and general welfare of the United States." There is no such provision as would authorize Congress to collect together the property of the country, under the name of revenue, for the purpose of dividing it equally or unequally among the States or the people.

Indeed, it is not probable that such an idea ever occurred to the States when they adopted the Constitution.... There would soon be but one taxing power, and that vested in a body of men far removed from the people, in which the farming and mechanic interests would scarcely be represented.

The States would gradually lose their purity as well as their independence; they would not dare to murmur at the proceedings of the General Government, lest they should lose their supplies; all would be merged in a practical consolidation, cemented by widespread corruption, which could only be eradicated by one of those bloody revolutions which occasionally overthrow the despotic systems of the Old World....

It was in view of these evils, together with the dangerous power wielded by the Bank of the United States and its repugnance to our Constitution, that I was induced to exert the power conferred upon me by the American people to prevent the continuance of that institution....

The lessons taught by the Bank of the United States cannot well be lost upon the American people. They will take care never again to place so tremendous a power in irresponsible hands....

And should I be spared to enter upon that retirement which is so suitable to my age and infirm health and so much desired by me in other respects, I shall not cease to invoke that beneficent Being to whose providence we are already so signally indebted for the continuance of His blessings on our beloved country.[57]

APPENDIX

Sir Alexander Fraser Tytler was an English historian, knighted Lord Woodhouselee. He wrote in *Universal History from the Creation of the World to the Beginning of the Eighteen Century* (Boston: Fetridge & Co., 1834; 1850):

With a very few exceptions...mankind has, in all ages, looked up to a supreme, intelligent, and omnipotent Being - the Author of our existence - the Creator and the Governor of the universe...

We have now traced Greece from her origin; from the rude and barbarous periods when she owed even the most necessary arts of life to foreign instructors, through every stage of her progress to the highest rank among the civilized nations of the earth.

We have seen the foundation and rise of her independent states; the vigorous perseverance by which they succeeded in shaking off the yoke of intolerable tyranny, and establishing a popular system of government; the alternate differences of these states from petty quarrels, the fruit of ambition and the love of power; while, at the same time they cordially united their strength and resources to oppose foreign hostilities, when such were formidable enough to threaten their liberties as a nation.

We have remarked the domestic disorders which sprang from the abuse of that freedom which these republics enjoyed; and, finally, that general corruption of manners which, tainting all the springs of public virtue, and annihilating patriotism, at length brought this illustrious nation entirely under subjection to a foreign yoke...

The miserable oppression which, according to all accounts of the ancient historians, the states of Greece sustained under their first governors, a set of tyrants, who owed their elevation to violence, and whose rule was subject to no control from existing laws or constitutional restraints, was assuredly a most justifiable motive on the part of the people for emancipating themselves from that state of servitude, and for abolishing entirely that worst of governments - a pure despotism.

It is therefore with pleasure we remark, in the early history of this nation, the noble exertion by which those states shook off the yoke of their tyrants, and established for themselves a new system of government on the just and rational basis of an equality of rights and privileges in all the members of the commonwealth.

We admit, without scruple, the belief that those new republics were framed by their virtuous legislators in the true spirit of patriotism...

The senate was, in theory, a wise institution, for it possessed the sole power of convoking the assemblies of the people, and of preparing all business that was to be the subject of discussion in those assemblies.

But, on the other hand, this senate being annually elected, its members were ever under the necessity of courting that people for their votes, and of flattering their prejudices and passions, by adopting and proposing measures which had no other end than to render themselves popular...

The guardians nominally of the people's rights, they were themselves the abject slaves of a corrupted populace. The wise purpose of the institution was thus utterly defeated...There were other radical defects in the constitution of Athens...The best apology that can be made for Solon is, that his intentions were good. He knew that a constitution purely democratic is an absolute chimera in politics.

He knew that the people are themselves incapable of exercising rule, and that, under one name or another, they must be led and controlled...

Whence it happened, that neither part of the public having its rights and privileges well defined, they were perpetually quarrelling about the limits of authority, and instead of a salutary and cordial cooperation for the general good of the state, it was an eternal contest for supremacy, and a mutual desire of each other's abasement...

They were perpetually divided into factions, which servilely ranked themselves under the banners of the contending demagogues; and these maintained their influence over their partisans by the most shameful corruption and bribery, of which the means were supplied alone by the plunder of the public money...

In every instance of election by the mass of a people - through the influence of those governors themselves, and by means the most opposite to a free and disinterested choice, by the basest corruption and bribery...

That they are chosen from the people affords no pledge that they will either be wiser men, or less influenced by selfish ambition, or the passion of tyrannizing; all experience goes to prove the contrary: and that the will of the many is in truth a mere chimera, and ultimately resolves into the will of one...

People flatter themselves that they have the sovereign power. These are, in fact, words without meaning. It is true they elect their governors; but how are these elections brought about?...

A pure and perfect democracy is a thing not attainable by man, constituted as he is of contending elements of vice and virtue, and ever mainly influenced by the predominant principle of self-interest...

In every regular state there must be a governing power, whose will regulates the community.

In the most despotic governments, that power is lodged in a single person, whose will is subject to no other control than that which arises from the fear of his own deposition. Of this we have an example in the Ottoman government, which approaches the nearest of any monarchy we know to a pure despotism.

But in most monarchies, the will of the person called the sovereign is limited by certain constitutional restraints which he cannot transgress with safety. In the British government the will of the prince is controlled by a parliament; in other limited monarchies, by a council of state, whose powers are acknowledged and defined...

The author of the "Spirit of Laws," a work which must ever be regarded as the production of a most enlightened mind, has built a great deal of plausible and ingenious reasoning on this general idea, that the three distinct forms of government, the MONARCHIAL, the DESPOTIC, and the REPUBLICAN, are influenced by three separate principles, upon which the whole system in each form is constructed, and on which it must depend for its support.

"The principle of the Monarchical form," says Montesquieu, "is HONOR; of the Despotical, FEAR; and of the Republican, VIRTUE:" a position which, if true, would at once determine to which of the three forms the preference ought to be given in speculating on their comparative degrees of merit.

In order to examine this important position, which is the foundation of a most elaborate theory, and from which the author draws conclusions deeply affecting the interests of society, we shall take the example of the Republic, with the nature and character of which form, we have had some opportunity of being acquainted from the preceding short sketch of the history of the Grecian commonwealths.

The ingenious author of an Essay on the History of Civil Society (Dr. Adam Ferguson, 1767) thus enlarges on the idea of M. Montesquieu: -

"In democracy," says he, "men must love equality; they must respect the rights of their fellow citizens; they must unite by the common ties of affection to the state...They must labor for the public without hope of profit. They must reject every attempt to create a personal dependence. Candor, force and elevation of mind, in short, are the props of democracy, and virtue is the principle required to its preservation."

A beautiful picture - a state indeed of consummate perfection!...

This beautiful picture...is nothing better than an utopian theory; a splendid chimera, descriptive of a state of society that never did, and never could exist; a republic not of men, but of angels.

For where, it may be asked, was that democracy ever found on earth, where, in the words of this description, men loved equality; were satisfied with the degree of consideration they could procure by their abilities fairly measured with those of an opponent, (a circumstance in itself utterly destructive of equality,) labored for the public without hope of profit, and rejected every attempt to create a personal dependence?

Did such a government ever exist, or, while society consists of human beings, is it possible that such ever should exist?

While man is a being instigated by the love of power - a passion visible in an infant, and common to us even with the inferior animals - he will seek personal superiority in preference to every matter of a general concern... Such is the true picture of man as a political agent...

The nature of a republican government gives to every member of the state an equal right to cherish views of ambition, and to aspire to the highest offices of the common wealth; it gives to every individual the same title with his fellows to aspire at the government of the whole...

The number of candidates excites rivalships, contentions, and factions. The glorious names of liberty and patriotism are always found effectual to rouse and inflame the multitude; rarely indeed to blind them to the real character and views of the demagogue, but ever sufficient to be a mask for their own love of tumult and the hatred of their superiors.

In such a state of society, how rare is genuine virtue; how singular the character of a truly disinterested patriot! He appears and he is treated as an imposter; he attempts to serve his country in its councils, or in offices; he is calumniated, reviled, and persecuted; he dies in disgrace or in banishment; and the same envy which maligned him living, embalms him dead, and showers encomiums on his memory, to depress and mortify the few surviving imitators of his virtues.

We have seen, from the history of the Grecian states, that a democracy has produced some splendid models of genuine patriotism in the persons of Aristides, Miltiades, and Cimon.

We have seen the reward that attended that character under this form of government, of which we are taught to believe that virtue is the principle...Montesquieu, 'Spirit of the Laws', has deduced such consequences as the following:

'That as in a democracy there is no occasion for the principle of honor, so in a monarchy virtue is not at all necessary; that under the latter government (monarchy) the state can subsist independently of the love of country, of the passion of true glory, and of every heroic virtue; that the laws supply the place of those virtues, and the state dispenses with, them; that under a monarchy, a virtuous man ought not to hold office; that public employments ought to be venal; and that crimes, if kept secret, are of no consequence.'...

The history of the states of Greece exhibits in its earliest period a very general diffusion of the patriotic spirit, and the love of ingenuous freedom. Those virtuous feelings became gradually corrupted as the nation advanced in power and splendor.

Selfish ambition and the desire of rule in the commonwealth came in place of the thirst for national glory; and at length the enthusiasm for freedom, which was at first the glowing character of the Grecian states, gave place to an enthusiasm of another kind...

Patriotism always exists in the greatest degree in rude nations, and in an early period of society.

Like all other affections and passions, it operates with the greatest force where it meets with the greatest difficulties.

It seems to be a virtue which grows from opposition; which subsists in its greatest vigor amidst turbulence and dangers; but in a state of ease and safety, as if wanting its appropriate nourishment, it languishes and decays.

We must not then wonder at that difference of patriotic character which distinguished the Greeks in the early ages of their history, from that by which they were known in their more advanced and more luxurious periods.

It is a law of nature to which no experience has ever furnished an exception, that the rising grandeur and opulence of a nation must be balanced by the decline of its heroic virtues.

When we find in the latter ages of the Grecian history, and in the declension of the Roman commonwealth and subsequent periods of the empire, no traces of that noble spirit of patriotism which excited our respect and admiration when they were infant and narrow establishments...

Wealth and ease and safety deny all exertion to heroic virtue; and in a society marked by these characteristics, such endowment can neither lead to power, to eminence, nor to fame.

Such was the situation of Greece, when, extending her conquests and importing both the wealth and the manners of foreign nations, she lost with her ancient poverty her ancient virtue.

Venality and corruption pervaded every department of her states, and became the spring of all public measures, which, instead of tending to the national welfare, had for their only object the gratification of the selfish passions of individuals.

Under these circumstances, it was no wonder that she should become an easy prey to a foreign power, which in fact rather purchased her in the market, than subdued her by force of arms.

APPENDIX

Alexis de Tocqueville wrote in *Democracy in America,* 1840, Vol. 2, The Second Part, Bk. 4, Ch. VI:

I had noted in my stay in the United States that a democratic state of society similar to the American model could lay itself open to the establishment of despotism with unusual ease...

It would debase men without tormenting them...

Men, all alike and equal, turned in upon themselves in a restless search for those petty, vulgar pleasures with which they fill their souls...

Above these men stands an immense and protective power...

It prefers its citizens to enjoy themselves provided they have only enjoyment in mind.

It restricts the activity of free will within a narrower range and gradually removes autonomy itself from each citizen...

Thus, the ruling power, having taken each citizen one by one into its powerful grasp...spreads its arms over the whole of society, covering the surface of social life with a network of petty, complicated, detailed, and uniform rules...

It does not break men's wills but it does soften, bend, and control them... It constantly opposes what actions they perform...

It inhibits, represses, drains, snuffs out, dulls so much effort that finally it reduces each nation to nothing more than a flock of timid and hardworking animals with the government as shepherd... a single, protective, and all-powerful government...

Individual intervention...is...suppressed...

It is...in the details that we run the risk of enslaving men.

For my part, I would be tempted to believe that freedom in the big things of life is less important than in the slightest...

Subjection in the minor things of life is obvious every day... It constantly irks them until they give up the exercise of their will...and enfeebles their spirit...

It will be useless to call upon those very citizens who have become so dependent upon central government to choose from time to time the representative of this government...

Increasing despotism in the administrative sphere... they reckon citizens are incompetent...

It is...difficult to imagine how men who have completely given up the habit of self-government could successfully choose those who should do it for them...

The vices of those who govern and the ineptitude of those governed would soon bring it to ruin and...revert to its abasement to one single master.

∞

APPENDIX

J OHN F. KENNEDY, JANUARY 30, 1961, ANNUAL

MESSAGE ON THE STATE OF THE UNION:
I will propose to the Congress within the next 14 days measures to offer tax incentives for sound plant investment. Our success in world affairs has long depended in part upon foreign confidence in our ability to pay. A series of executive orders, legislative remedies and cooperative efforts with our allies will get underway immediately - aimed at attracting foreign investment and travel to this country promoting American exports, at stable prices and with more liberal government guarantees and financing - curbing tax and customs loopholes that encourage undue spending of private dollars abroad. Organized and juvenile crimes cost the taxpayers millions of dollars each year.[58]

JOHN F. KENNEDY, FEBRUARY 2, 1961, PROGRAM FOR ECONOMIC RECOVERY & GROWTH:
An unbalanced economy does not produce a balanced budget. The Treasury's pocketbook suffers when the economy performs poorly. Lower incomes earned by households and corporations are reflected in lower Federal tax receipts. Special Tax Incentives to Investment - Expansion and modernization of the nation's productive plant is essential to accelerate economic growth and to improve the international competitive position of American industry.

Embodying modern research and technology in new facilities will advance productivity, reduce costs, and market new products. Moreover, an early stimulus to business investment will promote recovery and increase employment. Among the reforms of the Federal tax system which I expect to propose at a later date is a modification of the income tax laws to provide additional incentives for investment in plant and equipment. It should be possible to reform the tax system to stimulate economic growth, without reducing revenues and without violating the basic principles of fairness in taxation.

Price stability will also be aided by the adoption of a tax incentive plan mentioned earlier, which will encourage a higher rate of business investment in improved plants and equipment.

Neither will we seek to buy short-run economic gains by paying the price of excessive increases in the cost of living. Always a cruel tax upon the weak, inflation is now the certain road to a balance of payments crisis and the disruption of the international economy of the Western World.[59]

JOHN F. KENNEDY, FEBRUARY 6, 1961, MESSAGE ON GOLD & BALANCE OF PAYMENTS DEFICIT:

As a final means of holding or attracting foreign dollars, the Congress should enact a measure designed to unify the tax treatment accorded the earning assets of foreign central banks. At present, income derived by foreign central banks of issue from bankers acceptances and bank deposits is exempt from tax under section 861 of the Code.

Income from United States Government securities, however, is taxable to foreign central banks in the absence of applicable tax treaty provisions or a special ruling exempting a particular bank from taxation under particular circumstances. Suggested legislation will shortly be forthcoming. Abuse of 'tax havens' - Taxation of American Investment Abroad.

I shall recommend that the Congress enact legislation to prevent the abuse of foreign 'tax havens' by American capital abroad as a means of tax avoidance.

In addition, I have asked the Secretary of the Treasury to report by April 1 on whether present tax laws may be stimulating in undue amounts the flow of American capital to the industrial countries abroad through special preferential treatment, and to report further on what remedial action may be required.

But we shall not penalize legitimate private investment abroad, which will strengthen our trade and currency in future years.[60]

JOHN F. KENNEDY, FEBRUARY 13, 1961, TO NATIONAL INDUSTRIAL CONFERENCE BOARD:

An equally critical gap separates the tax revenues of a lagging economy from those which are potentially within our grasp: a gap of at least twelve billion dollars.

Even after we are able to launch every program necessary for national security and development, this amount of revenue would still leave a substantial surplus - a surplus essential to help defend our economy against inflation - and, equally important, a surplus that, when applied to the Federal debt, would free additional savings for business investment and expansion.

In short, there is no inevitable clash between the public and the private sectors-or between investment and consumption - nor, as I have said, between Government and business. All elements in our national economic growth are interdependent. Each must play its proper role, and that is the hope and the aim of this administration. Private surveys of machine tools used by manufacturers of general industrial equipment found less than half of these tools over 10 years old in 1949, but 2/3 over that age in 1958.

19 percent of our machine tools were found to be over 20 years old. Meanwhile, other countries have been lowering the average age of their fixed capital. The German example is the most spectacular-their proportion of capital equipment and plant under 5 years of age grew from one-sixth of the total in 1948 to two-fifths in 1957. All of these facts point in one direction: we must start now to provide additional stimulus to the modernization of American industrial plants.

Within the next few weeks, I shall propose to the Congress a new tax incentive for businesses to expand their normal investment in plant and equipment. Without strengthened programs for health, education, and science and research, the new modern plant would only be a hollow shell.

Many of these programs are within the province of State and local governments. Full recovery will increase the tax revenues that they so sorely need. But the Federal Government will have to pay its fair share of developing these human resources.[61]

JOHN F. KENNEDY, FEBRUARY 15, 1961, NEWS CONFERENCE:

In order to provide a stimulus to our economy I have provided, with the cooperation of the departments of the Government, for a speedup in programs using funds now available. Over $250 million, as we have said, will be distributed immediately under the GI dividend program.

There are $4 billion for tax refunds which are coming due. As soon as those who are available for these refunds can put their applications in, we will attempt to stimulate and improve and quicken distribution of these funds.[62]

JOHN F. KENNEDY, APRIL 20, 1961, SPECIAL MESSAGE TO CONGRESS ON TAXATION:

In meeting the demands of war finance, the individual income tax moved from a selective tax imposed on the wealthy to the means by which the great majority of our citizens participates in paying for well over one-half of our total budget receipts.

It is supplemented by the corporation income tax, which provides for another quarter of the total. Elimination of tax deferral privileges in developed countries and 'tax haven' deferral privileges in all countries.

Profits earned abroad by American firms operating through foreign subsidiaries are, under present tax laws, subject to United States tax only when they are returned to the parent company in the form of dividends. In some cases, this tax deferral has made possible indefinite postponement of the United States tax; and, in those countries where income taxes are lower than in the United States, the ability to defer the payment of U.S. tax by retaining income in the subsidiary companies provides a tax advantage for companies operating through overseas subsidiaries that is not available to companies operating solely in the United States.

Many American investors properly made use of this deferral in the conduct of their foreign investment. Though changing conditions now make continuance of the privilege undesirable, such change of policy implies no criticism of the investors who so utilize this privilege.

Withholding on Interest and Dividends.

Our system of combined withholding and voluntary reporting on wages and salaries under the individual income tax has served us well. Introduced during the war when the income tax was extended to millions of new taxpayers, the wage-withholding system has been one of the most important and successful advances in our tax system in recent times.

Initial difficulties were quickly overcome, and the new system helped the taxpayer no less than the tax collector.[63]

JOHN F. KENNEDY, MAY 16, 1961, LETTER TO THE EDITOR OF NEWSDAY, CONCERNING THE NATION'S RESPONSE TO THE COLD WAR:

Apparently the demands of the 'cold war' are not as dramatic, and thus not as well-identified, as the demands of the traditional 'shooting war' - such as rationing (which we do not need), a doubling of draft quotas (which would not help), or an increase in personal income taxes (which would only impede the recovery of our economic strength).[64]

JOHN F. KENNEDY, JANUARY 11, 1962, ANNUAL MESSAGE TO CONGRESS - THE STATE OF THE UNION:

Moreover, pleasant as it may be to bask in the warmth of recovery, let us not forget that we have suffered three recessions in the last 7 years. The time to repair the roof is when the sun is shining - by filling three basic gaps in our anti-recession protection.

We need: First, presidential standby authority, subject to congressional veto, to adjust personal income tax rates downward within a specified range and time, to slow down an economic decline before it has dragged us all down.[65]

JOHN F. KENNEDY, JANUARY 18, 1962, ANNUAL BUDGET MESSAGE TO CONGRESS, FISCAL YEAR 1963:

First, the President should be given standby discretionary authority, subject to congressional veto, to reduce personal income tax rates on clear evidence of economic need, for periods and by percentages set in the legislation.[66]

JOHN F. KENNEDY, JANUARY 22, 1962, MESSAGE TO CONGRESS - FIRST ECONOMIC REPORT:

To combat future recessions - to keep them short and shallow if they occur - I urge adoption of a three-part program for sustained prosperity, which will (1) provide stand-by power, subject to congressional veto, for temporary income tax reductions, (2) set up a stand-by program of public capital improvements, and (3) strengthen the unemployment insurance system.

A Program for Sustained Prosperity - Recurrent recessions have thrown the postwar American economy off stride at a time when the economies of other major industrial countries have moved steadily ahead. To improve our future performance I urge the Congress to join with me in erecting a defense-in-depth against future recessions.

The basic elements of this defense are (1) Presidential stand-by authority for prompt, temporary income tax reductions, (2) Presidential stand-by authority for capital improvements expenditures, and (3) a permanent strengthening of the unemployment compensation system. These three measures parallel important proposals of the Commission on Money and Credit, whose further recommendations are treated under the next heading.

Stand-by TAX REDUCTION authority.

First, I recommend the enactment of stand-by authority under which the President, subject to veto by the Congress, could make prompt temporary reductions in the rates of the individual income tax to combat recessions, as follows:

(1) Before proposing a temporary tax reduction, the President must make a finding that such action is required to meet the objectives of the Employment Act.

(2) Upon such finding, the President would submit to Congress a proposed temporary uniform reduction in all individual income tax rates. The proposed temporary rates may not be more than five percentage points lower than the rates permanently established by the Congress.

(3) This change would take effect 30 days after submission,

unless rejected by a joint resolution of the Congress.

(4) It would remain in effect for 6 months, subject to revision or renewal by the same process or extension by a joint resolution of the Congress.

(5) If the Congress were not in session, a Presidentially proposed tax adjustment would automatically take effect but would terminate 30 days after the Congress reconvened. Extension would require a new proposal by the President, which would be subject to congressional veto.

A temporary reduction of individual income tax rates across the board can be a powerful safeguard against recession. It would reduce the annual rate of tax collections by $2 billion per percentage point, or a maximum of $10 billion - $1 billion per point, or a $5-billion maximum, for six months-at present levels of income.

These figures should be measured against the costs they are designed to forestall: -the tens of billions of potential output that run to waste in recession; -the pain and frustration of the millions whom recessions throw out of work; -the Budget deficits of $12.4 billion in fiscal 1959 or $7.0 billion this year.

The proposed partial tax suspension would launch a prompt counterattack on the cumulative forces of recession. It would be reflected immediately in lower withholding deductions and higher take-home pay for millions of Americans. Markets for consumer goods and services would promptly feel the stimulative influence of the tax suspension.

It would offer strong support to the economy for a timely interval, while preserving the revenue-raising powers of our tax system in prosperity and the wise traditional procedures of the Congress for making permanent revisions and reforms in the system. I am not asking the Congress to delegate its power to levy taxes, but to authorize a temporary and emergency suspension of taxes by the President 'subject to the check of Congressional veto' in situations where time is of the essence.

Later this year, I shall present to the Congress a major program of tax reform. This broad program will re-examine tax rates and the definition of the income tax base. It will be aimed at the simplification of our tax structure, the equal treatment of equally situated persons, and the strengthening of incentives for individual effort and for productive investment.

The momentum of our economy has been restored. This momentum must be maintained, if the full potential of our free economy is to be released in the service of the Nation and the world. In this Report: I have proposed a program to sustain our prosperity and accelerate our growth - in short, to realize our economic potential. In this undertaking, I ask the support of the Congress and the American people.

JOHN F. KENNEDY, APRIL 18, 1962, NEWS CONFERENCE:

In the pursuit of these objectives, we have fostered a responsible wage policy aimed at holding increases within the confines of productivity gains.

We have encouraged monetary policies aimed at making borrowed capital available at reasonable cost; preparing a new transportation policy aimed at providing increased freedom of competition at lower costs; proposed a new trade expansion bill to gain for our industries increased access to foreign markets; proposed an eight percent income tax credit to reward investment in new equipment and machinery; and proceeded to modernize administratively Treasury Department's guidelines on the depreciable lives of capital assets; and, finally, taken a host of other legislative and administrative actions to foster the kind of economic recovery which would improve both profits and incentives to invest.[68]

JOHN F. KENNEDY, APRIL 30, 1962, ON 50TH ANNIVERSARY OF U.S. CHAMBER OF COMMERCE:

We have worked to establish the responsible view that we take of our role in the economy, and I do not think the record of our decisions, taken in totality, has been one to suggest that we are not responsive to the problems of business. I will point to our efforts in the field of inflation, to the balance of payments, to the transportation policy, for example, recently enunciated, as tenders of this concern I expect to be able to point soon to more realistic income tax guidelines on the depreciable lives of business assets, and to the eight-percent tax credit for investment in equipment and machinery, which has been proposed and is now being considered by the Senate.[69]

JOHN F. KENNEDY, MAY 8, 1962, TO THE PRESIDENT OF THE SENATE, LYNDON B. JOHNSON, AND SPEAKER OF THE HOUSE, JOHN MCCORMACK, ON STANDBY AUTHORITY TO REDUCE INCOME TAXES:

Dear Mr._____: I transmit herewith, for the consideration of the Congress, a draft and a technical explanation of a bill which would give to the President, subject to Congressional disapproval, stand-by discretionary authority to reduce personal income tax rates when economic circumstances require such action.

This bill implements one of the three proposals advanced in my Economic Report for bolstering the Government's ability to pursue effectively the objectives of the Employment Act of 1946. I have previously sent to the Congress draft legislation to carry out the other two recommended economic stabilizers: a strengthened and permanent unemployment compensation program and a stand-by capital improvements program designed to become effective in the early stages of economic recession.

Under the Employment Act of 1946, the Congress declared that... it is the continuing policy and responsibility of the federal Government to use all practicable means consistent with its needs and obligations and other essential considerations of national policy...to promote maximum employment, production, and purchasing power.' Since 1946 the stability of our economy has been substantially greater than in the decade preceding the war, but the record has not been good enough.

Recessions which began in 1948, 1953, 1957, and 1960 have resulted in the loss of tens of billions of dollars of potential output and frustration, privation, and degradation for millions of workers who, through recessions, have been unemployed.

These recurrent recessions have thrown the postwar American economy off its stride at a time when the economies of other major industrial nations have moved steadily ahead, thus contributing substantially to the failure of the American economy to grow at a pace equal to that of our principal competitors.

I ask for stand-by authority for prompt, temporary income tax reductions as one means of improving our future performance in meeting the goals of the Employment Act. As I said in my Economic Report, 'Our fiscal system and budget policy already contribute to economic stability, to a much greater degree than before the war. But the time is ripe, and the need apparent to equip the Government to act more promptly, more flexibly, and more forcefully to stabilize the economy - to carry out more effectively its charge under the Employment Act.'

Authority to introduce promptly a temporary reduction of individual tax rates across the board would constitute a powerful addition to the equipment available to the Government for this purpose. At present income levels, the proposal would grant authority to reduce individual income tax collections at an annual rate of $2 billion per percentage point, or a maximum of $10 billion if the full five percentage point reduction permitted by the bill is put into effect.

The proposed partial temporary tax suspension would be reflected immediately in lower withholding deductions and higher take-home pay for millions of Americans. Markets for consumer goods and services would promptly feel this stimulating influence of the tax suspension. Thus, strong support would be offered to the economy for a timely interval. The revenue-raising powers of our tax system and the traditional procedures of the Congress for revision and reform of the system would be entirely preserved under this legislation. My proposal, as contained in the draft bill does not ask the Congress to delegate its power to levy taxes.

It asks only for authorization for a temporary and emergency reduction of income tax rates by the President, subject to Congressional disapproval, in situations where prompt action, whether or not the Congress is in session, is essential.

The form of the income tax reduction would be provided for in advance by Congress; it would not be determined by the President. By the term of the draft legislation the fixed statutory rates may be reduced by not more than five percentage points and the period of tax reduction would be limited to six months, unless extended by a new plan within the procedures prescribed in the bill. In no event can the period of uninterrupted tax reduction exceed one year without specific affirmative Congressional action.

The draft bill authorizes the President to terminate the period of tax reduction on a date earlier than that specified if he finds that a reduction in tax rates is no longer needed. The draft proposal thus offers a practical plan for cooperative governmental action. Enactment of the proposed legislation would provide the basic legislative determination to use a temporary reduction in the individual income tax rates when economic circumstances require such action, while arming the President with a practical means of implementing the Congressional will.

The responsibility to act promptly would be the President's, but Congress would have the opportunity to disapprove the proposed reduction. A plan of tax reduction would, in general, take effect 31 days after submission by the President, but only if in the course of this period Congress does not disapprove the plan by concurrent resolution. Since the proposed legislation calls for prompt action to achieve its objectives, however, the provisions of the bill permit submission of plans of tax reduction when Congress is adjourned sine die.

If such a plan is submitted when Congress is adjourned sine die, it would take effect in accordance with its terms, but the period during which the tax rate reduction is in effect would terminate not later than the 31st calendar day following the date on which Congress convenes, unless it were continued under the terms of a new plan submitted by the President on that date.

The President would be authorized to request one extension of a period of tax reduction; only specific action by Congress could continue uninterrupted temporary tax reduction beyond a maximum of one year. Thus the proposed legislation combines assurance of Congressional control with provision for the flexibility of action needed to achieve the objectives of maximum employment and output, economic stability, and growth.

JOHN F. KENNEDY, JUNE 7, 1962, NEWS CONFERENCE:

Taxation: In the first place, our tax structure as presently weighted exerts too heavy a drain on a prospering economy, compared, for example, to the net drain in competing Common Market nations. If the United States were now working at full employment and full capacity, this would produce a budget surplus at present taxation rates of about $8 billion this year. It indicates what a heavy tax structure we have, and it also indicates the effects that this heavy tax structure has on an economy moving out of a recession period. We saw that after the '58 recession, we've seen it after the '60 recession in the last months. We have proposed, therefore, the following:

ONE: A $1,300 million tax credit of eight percent on new investment in machinery and equipment, which will increase the typical rate of potential profits on modern plant expansion in this country to the same extent, for example, as a 20 point reduction in corporate income taxes, from 52 to 32 percent on the profits to be realized from a new 10-year asset. The tax bill containing this stimulus and offsetting revenue measures has been before the Congress for well over a year. And I am hopeful, particularly, that it can be passed very shortly, because one of the areas of concern in the economy has been the slowness of plant investment, and I think that if we can settle this matter of the tax credit quickly, I think it can have a most stimulating effect on new plant investment this year.

TWO: Administrative revision of the Internal Revenue guidelines on the economic life of depreciable assets, to make them more realistic and flexible in terms of actual replacement practices. These revisions to be issued within the next month will also make over $1 billion in added cash reserves available for additional business investment and, thus, these two actions combined, which we hope will be taken in the next 30 days, constitute in effect a tax cut for American business of over $2.5 billion.

THREE: A comprehensive tax reform bill which in no way overlaps the pending tax credit and loophole-closing bill offered a year ago will be offered for action by the next Congress, making effective as of January 1 of next year an across-the-board reduction in personal and corporate income tax rates which will not be wholly offset by other reforms-in other words, a net tax reduction.

FOUR: I have asked the Congress to provide standby tax reduction authority to make certain as recommended by the eminent Commission on Money and Credit, that this tool could be used instantly and effectively should a new recession threaten to engulf us. The House Ways and Means Committee has been busy with other important measures, but there is surely more cause now than ever before for making such authority available.

FIVE: I have asked the Congress to repeal the 10- percent transportation tax on train and bus travel, resulting in a tax saving of $90 million a year, and to reduce it to five percent on airlines. Action on this tax package will provide our economy with all the stimulus and safeguards now deemed necessary, and I hope such action will be forthcoming.... I have full confidence in the basic strength and economic potential of this country and the free world.

We in the United States, business, labor, and the government, all of us working together, rather than at cross purposes, must rise to our responsibilities to maintain the forward thrust of our economy. The economic productivity and potential of the United States is the heart of our strength. Unemployment last month declined. Consumer income has been rising rapidly. New homes are being built at a remarkable rate. And this administration intends to do its full share of the task required to realize our full economic potential.

Q. Mr. President, I take it from your statement that you have no intention of recommending a tax cut to take effect before next year. Would you confirm that? And also tell us if you can envision any circumstances which would require tax reduction before next year?

THE PRESIDENT. I think my statement goes into the various tax proposals that we make in some detail. Of course, this is our best judgment at this time. Of course, if new circumstances brought a new situation, then we would have to make other judgments. But this is our judgment and we believe that this is the most responsible and effective line to take. And I think that if we get action in all the areas which I have described - and they are all very possible - that we can provide a good sustaining lift to the economy.

Q. Mr. President, in the same subject, can you discuss any thinking on rates or how far the reduction will go that you intend to propose in January? And second, sir, if you don't get some of these provisions or proposals which you regard as quite vital, are you thinking in terms of asking Congress to return in the fall if they don't pass them, say, by mid-September?

THE PRESIDENT. Well, I think the tax-the proposed tax bill you are talking about for next January, the work on it should be completed later in the summer. So at that time I think we could discuss it in more detail. On the other matter, I would-already it has passed the House. The depreciation we can do by administrative action, and we are going to do that, and, as I say, that amounts to over $1 billion. That will be completed in the next 30 days. It has already been done in the textile industry. But the whole job will be completed in the next 30 days.

The other bill, the tax credit, has passed the House. It is now in the Senate finance Committee. It can be of most valuable assistance in the area where our economy has had the most difficulty, and that is on the question of plant investment. So that if you could put these two together, as I said, it amounts to $2,500 million, and I think would be of great assistance to the economy. So I am very hopeful that the Senate will act on this legislation. If they do not, of course we will have to take a look at the situation. But this bill was proposed last year, and a year now has gone by, and now we are going through other months. I think the very fact that some companies are uncertain as to whether they are going to get the tax credit does have a depressing effect upon their investment plans.[71]

JOHN F. KENNEDY, JUNE 14, 1962, NEWS CONFERENCE, STATE DEPARTMENT AUDITORIUM:

Q. Mr. President, while most of business certainly doesn't oppose your income tax reduction plan, many businessmen have said if you really want to give business and the economy a shot in the arm, that you should give them a better break on depreciation, tax write-offs, and so forth. Now I know that a new schedule is coming out, I think within the month, but in addition to that, do you contemplate anything in this area that will help?

THE PRESIDENT. We are going to, as I said before, by the 6th of July come forward with the quicker depreciation write-offs under schedule f for $1,200 million. That could have been done any time in the last 15 to 20 years. We have been working on it now for a year. That is going to be important. In addition, under the tax bill itself, it provides very important assistance to business if we are able to secure its passage by the Senate. And, of course, the third provision of the tax bill is the standby tax authorities in case unemployment begins to move up, which will permit us to have a temporary tax reduction in many brackets. All those I regard as very important. Reporter: Thank you, Mr. President.[72]

JOHN F. KENNEDY, JULY 6, 1962, TO DAVID ROCKEFELLER ON BALANCE OF PAYMENTS QUESTION:

Fully aware of the need you cite for increased investment, we have proposed a new tax credit which will increase the profitability of investments in new equipment and machinery by a far greater margin for every dollar of revenue foregone than alternative proposals. This will be supplemented by revision of the Treasury's depreciation rules which will give businessmen both far more flexibility and more realistic, up-to-date guidelines for charging off the cost of depreciable assets.

The combined impact of these two moves is, in effect, a 'tax cut' for American businessmen who modernize of more than $2.5 billion, a lessening of the squeeze on profits, a greater supply of funds for investment and a greater incentive to invest them. In addition, the 'thoroughgoing overhaul of the Nation's tax system' to which you refer is planned for next year, effecting a net reduction in the burden of both corporate and personal income taxes.[73]

JOHN F. KENNEDY, AUGUST 13, 1962, REPORT ON THE STATE OF THE NATIONAL ECONOMY:

Such a bill will be presented to the Congress for action next year. It will include an across the board, top to bottom cut in both corporate and personal income taxes. It will include long-needed tax reform that logic and equity demand. And it will date that cut in taxes to take effect as of the start of next year, January 1963. The billions of dollars this bill will place in the hands of the consumer and our businessmen will have both immediate and permanent benefits to our economy. Every dollar released from taxation that is spent or invested will help create a new job and a new salary. And these new jobs and new salaries can create other jobs and other salaries and more customers and more growth for an expanding American economy.[74]

JOHN F. KENNEDY, NOVEMBER 20, 1962, NEWS CONFERENCE:

Q. Mr. President, are you going to ask Congress for a $10 billion income tax cut in January, as recommended by your Labor-Management Policy Committee?

THE PRESIDENT. The question of the tax cut is going to be discussed in the administration in the next 10 days, and we'll have recommendations to make the first part of January. Until then, I'll have to withhold, until we finally decide what we are going to do - the amounts, and where the cut will come. The final and best means of strengthening demand among consumers and business is to reduce the burden on private income and the deterrents to private initiative which are imposed by our present tax system; and this administration pledged itself last summer to an across-the-board, top-to-bottom cut in personal and corporate income taxes to be enacted and become effective in 1963.

I am not talking about a 'quickie' or a temporary tax cut, which would be more appropriate if a recession were imminent. Nor am I talking about giving the economy a mere shot in the arm, to ease some temporary complaint.

I am talking about the accumulated evidence of the last 5 years that our present tax system, developed as it was, in good part, during World War II to restrain growth, exerts too heavy a drag on growth in peace time; that it siphons out of the private economy too large a share of personal and business purchasing power; that it reduces the financial incentives for personal effort, investment, and risk-taking. In short, to increase demand and lift the economy, the Federal Government's most useful role is not to rush into a program of excessive increases in public expenditures, but to expand the incentives and opportunities for private expenditures.

Under these circumstances, any new tax legislation - and you can understand that under the comity which exists in the United States Constitution whereby the Ways and Means Committee in the House of Representatives have the responsibility of initiating this legislation, that the details of any proposal should wait on the meeting of the Congress in January. But you can understand that under these circumstances, in general, that any new tax legislation enacted next year should meet the following three tests:

FIRST, it should reduce net taxes by a sufficiently early date and a sufficiently large amount to do the job required. Early action could give us extra leverage, added results, and important insurance against recession. Too large a tax cut, of course, could result in inflation and insufficient future revenues - but the greatest danger is a tax cut too little or too late to be effective.

SECOND, the new tax bill must increase private consumption as well as investment. Consumers are still spending between 92 and 94 percent of their after-tax income, as they have every year since 1950. But that after-tax income could and should be greater, providing stronger markets for the products of American industry. When consumers purchase more goods, plants use more of their capacity, men are hired instead of laid off, investment increases and profits are high. Corporate tax rates must also be cut to increase incentives and the availability of investment capital. T

he Government has already taken major steps this year to reduce business tax liability and to stimulate the modernization, replacement, and expansion of our productive plant and equipment. We have done this through the 1962 investment tax credit and through the liberalization of depreciation allowances - two essential parts of our first step in tax revision which amounted to a 10 percent reduction in corporate income taxes worth $2.5 billion. Now we need to increase consumer demand to make these measures fully effective- demand which will make more use of existing capacity and thus increase both profits and the incentive to invest. In fact, profits after taxes would be at least 15 percent higher today if we were operating at full employment.

For all these reasons, next year's tax bill should reduce personal as well as corporate income taxes, for those in the lower brackets, who are certain to spend their additional take-home pay, and for those in the middle and upper brackets, who can thereby be encouraged to undertake additional efforts and enabled to invest more capital.

THIRD, the new tax bill should improve both the equity and the simplicity of our present tax system. This means the enactment of long-needed tax reforms, a broadening of the tax base and the elimination or modification of many special tax privileges. These steps are not only needed to recover lost revenue and thus make possible a larger cut in present rates; they are also tied directly to our goal of greater growth.

For the present patchwork of special provisions and preferences lightens the tax load of some only at the cost of placing a heavier burden on others. It distorts economic judgments and channels an undue amount of energy into efforts to avoid tax liabilities. It makes certain types of less productive activity more profitable than other more valuable undertakings. All this inhibits our growth and efficiency, as well as considerably complicating the work of both the taxpayer and the Internal Revenue Service.

These various exclusions and concessions have been justified in part as a means of overcoming oppressively high rates in the upper brackets - and a sharp reduction in those rates, accompanied by base-broadening, loophole-closing measures, would properly make the new rates not only lower but also more widely applicable. Surely this is more equitable on both counts.

Those are the three tests which the right kind of bill must meet and I am confident that the enactment of the right bill next year will in due course increase our gross national product by several times the amount of taxes actually cut. Profit margins will be improved and both the incentive to invest and the supply of internal funds for investment will be increased.

There will be new interest in taking risks, in increasing productivity, in creating new jobs and new products for long-term economic growth. Other national problems, moreover, will be aided by full employment. It will encourage the location of new plants in areas of labor surplus and provide new jobs for workers that we are retraining and facilitate the adjustment which will be necessary under our new trade expansion bill and reduce a number of government expenditures.

It will not, I'm confident, revive an inflationary spiral or adversely affect our balance of payments. If the economy today were operating close to capacity levels with little unemployment, or if a sudden change in our military requirements should cause a scramble for men and resources, then I would oppose tax reductions as irresponsible and inflationary; and I would not hesitate to recommend a tax increase, if that were necessary.

But our resources and manpower are not being fully utilized; the general level of prices has been remarkably stable; and increased competition, both at home and abroad, along with increased productivity will help keep both prices and wages within appropriate limits. The same is true of our balance of payments.

While rising demand will expand imports, new investment in more efficient productive facilities will aid exports and a new economic climate could both draw capital from abroad and keep capital here at home. It will also put us in a better position, if necessary, to use monetary tools to help our international accounts.

But, most importantly, confidence in the dollar in the long run rests on confidence in America, in our ability to meet our economic commitments and reach our economic goals. In a worldwide conviction that we are not drifting from recession to recession with no answer, the substantial improvement in our balance of payments position in the last 2 years makes it clear that nothing could be more foolish than to restrict our growth merely to minimize that particular problem, because a slowdown in our economy will feed that problem rather than diminish it.

On the contrary, European governmental and financial authorities with almost total unanimity, far from threatening to withdraw gold, have urged us to cut taxes in order to expand our economy, attract more capital, and increase confidence in our future. But what concerns most Americans about a tax cut, I know, is not the deficit in our balance of payments but the deficit in our Federal budget. When

I announced in April of 1961 that this kind of comprehensive tax reform would follow the bill enacted this year, I had hoped to present it in an atmosphere of a balanced budget.

But it has been necessary to augment sharply our nuclear and conventional forces, to step up our efforts in space, to meet the increased cost of servicing the national debt and meeting our obligations, established by law, to veterans. These expenditure increases, let me stress, constitute practically all of the increases which have occurred under this administration, the remainder having gone to fight the recession we found in industry - mostly through the supplemental employment bill - and in agriculture. We shall, therefore, neither postpone our tax cut plans nor cut into essential national security programs.

This administration is determined to protect America's security and survival and we are also determined to step up its economic growth. I think we must do both. Our true choice is not between tax reduction, on the one hand, and the avoidance of large Federal deficits on the other. It is increasingly clear that no matter what party is in power, so long as our national security needs keep rising, an economy hampered by restrictive tax rates will never produce enough revenue to balance our budget just as it will never produce enough jobs or enough profits. Surely the lesson of the last decade is that budget deficits are not caused by wild-eyed spenders but by slow economic growth and periodic recessions, and any new recession would break all deficit records.

In short, it is a paradoxical truth that tax rates are too high today and tax revenues are too low and the soundest way to raise the revenues in the long run is to cut the rates now. The experience of a number of European countries and Japan have borne this out.

This country's own experience with tax reduction in 1954 has borne this out. And the reason is that only full employment can balance the budget, and tax reduction can pave the way to that employment. The purpose of cutting taxes now is not to incur a budget deficit, but to achieve the more prosperous, expanding economy which can bring a budget surplus. I repeat: our practical choice is not between a tax-cut deficit and a budgetary surplus. It is between two kinds of deficits:

a chronic deficit of inertia, as the unwanted result of inadequate revenues and a restricted economy; or a temporary deficit of transition, resulting from a tax cut designed to boost the economy, increase tax revenues, and achieve - and I believe this can be done-a budget surplus.

The first type of deficit is a sign of waste and weakness; the second reflects an investment in the future. Nevertheless, as Chairman Mills of the House Ways and Means Committee pointed out this week, the size of the deficit is to be regarded with concern, and tax reduction must be accompanied, in his words, by 'increased control of the rises in expenditures.' This is precisely the course we intend to follow in 1963.

Q. There has been much talk in Washington and elsewhere of reductions in personal income tax rates to 15 percent for the lowest brackets, and 65 for the highest brackets, in personal income taxes, and for a reduction in corporate rates to 47 percent. What many of these questioners would like to know is, are those figures generally in the ball park?

THE PRESIDENT. This legislation is going to have very difficult traveling at best, and I would suggest giving it at least the most favorable start we can, as I said in my speech, by permitting Mr. Dillon to present this before the Ways and Means Committee in January. So that I would suggest that the details of the tax reduction should wait upon presentation to the Ways and Means Committee. There might be something for everybody, though.[75]

JOHN F. KENNEDY, JANUARY 14, 1963, ANNUAL MESSAGE TO CONGRESS ON STATE OF THE UNION:

To achieve these greater gains, one step, above all, is essential-the enactment this year of a substantial reduction and revision in Federal income taxes. For it is increasingly clear-to those in Government, business, and labor who are responsible for our economy's success - that our obsolete tax system exerts too heavy a drag on private purchasing power, profits, and employment.

Designed to check inflation in earlier years, it now checks growth instead. It discourages extra effort and risk. It distorts the use of resources. It invites recurrent recessions, depresses our Federal revenues, and causes chronic budget deficits. Now, when the inflationary pressures of the war and the post-war years no longer threaten, and the dollar commands new respect - now, when no military crisis strains our resources - now is the time to act.

We cannot afford to be timid or slow. For this is the most urgent task confronting the Congress in 1963. In an early message, I shall propose a permanent reduction in tax rates which will lower liabilities by $13.5 billion. Of this, $11 billion results from reducing individual tax rates, which now range between 20 and 91 percent, to a more sensible range of 14 to 65 percent, with a split in the present first bracket. Two and one-half billion dollars results from reducing corporate tax rates, from 52 percent-which gives the Government today a majority interest in profits - to the permanent pre-Korean level of 47 percent.

This is in addition to the more than $2 billion cut in corporate tax liabilities resulting from last year's investment credit and depreciation reform. To achieve this reduction within the limits of a manageable budgetary deficit, I urge: first, that these cuts be phased over 3 calendar years, beginning in 1963 with a cut of some $6 billion at annual rates; second, that these reductions be coupled with selected structural changes, beginning in 1964, which will broaden the tax base, end unfair or unnecessary preferences, remove or lighten certain hardships, and in the net offset some $3.5 billion of the revenue loss; and third, that budgetary receipts at the outset be increased by $1.5 billion a year, without any change in tax liabilities, by gradually shifting the tax payments of large corporations to a . more current time schedule.

This combined program, by increasing the amount of our national income, will in time result in still higher Federal revenues. It is a fiscally responsible program - the surest and the soundest way of achieving in time a balanced budget in a balanced full employment economy. This net reduction in tax liabilities of $10 billion will increase the purchasing power of American families and business enterprises in every tax bracket, with greatest increase going to our low-income consumers. It will, in addition, encourage the initiative and risk-taking on which our free system depends - induce more investment, production, and capacity use - help provide the 2 million new jobs we need every year - and reinforce the American principle of additional reward for additional effort. I do not say that a measure for tax reduction and reform is the only way to achieve these goals.

-NO doubt a massive increase in Federal spending could also create jobs and growth-but, in today's setting, private consumers, employers, and investors should be given a full opportunity first.

-NO doubt a temporary tax cut could provide a spur to our economy - but a long run problem compels a long-run solution.

-NO doubt a reduction in either individual or corporation taxes alone would be of great help-but corporations need customers and job seekers need jobs.

-NO doubt tax reduction without reform would sound simpler and more attractive to many - but our growth is also hampered by a host of tax inequities and special preferences which have distorted the flow of investment.

-AND, finally, there are no doubt some who would prefer to put off a tax cut in the hope that ultimately an end to the cold war would make possible an equivalent cut in expenditures - but that end is not in view and to wait for it would be costly and self-defeating. In submitting a tax program which will, of course, temporarily increase the deficit but can ultimately end it - and in recognition of the need to control expenditures - I will shortly submit a fiscal 1964 administrative budget which, while allowing for needed rises in defense, space, and fixed interest charges, holds total expenditures for all other purposes below this year's level.

This requires the reduction or postponement of many desirable programs, the absorption of a large part of last year's Federal pay raise through personnel and other economies, the termination of certain installations and projects, and the substitution in several programs of private for public credit.

But I am convinced that the enactment this year of tax reduction and tax reform overshadows all other domestic problems in this Congress. For we cannot for long lead the cause of peace and freedom, if we ever cease to set the pace here at home.[76]

JOHN F. KENNEDY, JANUARY 17, 1963, ANNUAL BUDGET MESSAGE TO CONGRESS, FISCAL YEAR 1964:

My tax proposals include substantial permanent reductions in individual and corporation income tax rates as well as a number of important structural changes designed to encourage economic growth, increase the equity of our tax system, and simplify our tax laws and administration. Some reductions in rates would start in the calendar year 1963. The remainder of the program, including additional income tax rate reductions for both individuals and corporations, together with structural reforms and other revisions, would become effective in 1964 and 1965.

The entire tax program, which I will shortly recommend to the Congress as a single comprehensive measure, is a major step in the effort to strengthen and improve our tax system. The recommended tax rate reductions extend over every bracket of individual income tax rates. The largest proportionate tax reductions, measured as a percentage of tax liability and in relation to the total revenue loss to the Government, are proposed for those with the lowest incomes. The recommendations also provide for more equitable tax treatment through changes affecting the tax base and remove certain tax concessions that will no longer be appropriate. In every respect, the proposals are consistent with generally accepted American standards of fair play, while at the same time they are designed to provide needed economic incentives.

The proposed corporation income tax reductions are supplemented by recommended structural changes to strengthen the position of small business and to correct distortions in the existing structure which result in the misallocation of energy and resources. Part of the loss in Treasury tax collections attributable to rate reductions would be offset by the introduction of a gradual program to place payment of income tax liabilities of large corporations on a more current basis.

The proposed tax program, when fully effective, would reduce tax liabilities by about $10 billion compared to the present tax system, when both calculations are based on the same calendar year 1963 levels of income. Incomes, however, will not be the same under the new tax program. Because my proposals incorporate lower rates of taxation as well as tax reform measures, they will stimulate economic activity and so raise the levels of personal and corporate income as to yield within a few years an increased - not a reduced - flow of revenues to the Federal Government. Revenue estimates. - Estimates of Federal receipts must be based upon specific economic assumptions.

The revenue estimates in this budget assume a gross national product in the calendar year 1963 of $578 billion. This figure is the midpoint of a range of expectation which extends $5 billion on each side. The anticipated rise in the gross national product from the calendar 1962 level of $554 billion takes into account some initial economic stimulus expected from adoption of my tax recommendations.

That part of the proposed reductions in tax rates becoming effective in calendar 1963 would, by itself, reduce fiscal 1964 tax revenues by some $5.3 billion. Placing the payment of corporate income taxes on a more current basis, however, will reduce this revenue loss, as will the initial spur provided by the tax program to private production and incomes. Taking account of these factors, the net revenue loss in fiscal 1964 from my tax program is estimated at $2.7 billion. Despite this revenue loss, administrative budget receipts are estimated to rise by $1.4 billion in fiscal year 1964 because of the anticipated expansion in economic activity.

As we learned again this past year, there are many uncertainties in estimating economic developments and Federal revenues so far ahead. If the economy grows more strongly and quickly than we now foresee, revenues would be higher than now estimated. On the other hand - although I consider this unlikely if my proposals are approved promptly by the Congress - slower growth in the economy would be accompanied by smaller revenues.

This would indeed be unfortunate, both because of the effect on Government finances, and because of the lost opportunities and the human misfortune that would accompany a sluggish economy and growing unemployment. Tax extension. - Legislation is needed to extend certain excise tax rates for another year. Without such legislation, these tax rates would be reduced or would expire on July 1, 1963, resulting in a revenue loss in fiscal year 1964 of $1.6 billion.

Under present law, the maximum corporation income tax rate would be reduced from 52 percent to 47 percent on July 1, 1963. My legislative proposals include an extension of the 52 percent maximum rate for six months, but provide, in accordance with my tax program, for certain changes in the tax treatment of corporations which will also be applicable to that period.[77]

JOHN F. KENNEDY, JANUARY 21, 1963, ANNUAL MESSAGE TO CONGRESS, ECONOMIC REPORT:

A year ago, there was widespread consensus that economic recovery in 1962, while not matching the swift pace of 1961, would continue at a high rate. But the pace slackened more than expected as the average quarterly change in GNP was only $6 billion in 1962 against $13 billion in 1961.

The underlying forces in the private economy - no longer buttressed by the exuberant demand of the postwar decade, yet still thwarted by income tax rates bred of war and inflation - failed to provide the stimulus needed for more vigorous expansion. While housing and government purchases rose about as expected and consumer buying moved up rather well relative to income, increases in business investment fell short of expectations.

Yet, buttressed by the policies and programs already listed, the momentum of the expansion was strong enough to carry the economy safely past the shoals of a sharp break in the stock market, a drop in the rate of inventory accumulation, and a wave of pessimism in early summer. As the year ended, the economy was still moving upward. The Responsible Citizen and Tax Reduction In this situation, the citizen serves his country's interest by supporting income tax reductions.

For through the normal processes of the market economy, tax reduction can be the constructive instrument for harmonizing public and private interests: -The taxpayer as consumer, pursuing his own best interest and that of his family, can turn his tax savings into a higher standard of living, and simultaneously into stronger markets for the producer. -The taxpayer as producer - businessman or farmer - responding to the profit opportunities he finds in fuller markets and lower tax rates, can simultaneously create new jobs for workers and larger markets for the products of other factories, farms, and mines.

Tax reduction thus sets off a process that can bring gains for everyone, gains won by marshaling resources that would otherwise stand idle-workers without jobs and farm and factory capacity without markets. Yet many taxpayers seem prepared to deny the nation the fruits of tax reduction because they question the financial soundness of reducing taxes when the Federal budget is already in deficit. Let me make clear why, in today's economy, fiscal prudence and responsibility call for tax reduction even if it temporarily enlarges the Federal deficit - why reducing taxes is the best way open to us to increase revenues.

Our choice is not the oversimplified one sometimes posed, between tax reduction and a deficit on one hand and a budget easily balanced by prudent management on the other. If the projected 1964 Federal cash deficit of $10.3 billion did not allow for a $2.7 billion loss in receipts owing to the new tax program, the projected deficit would be $7.6 billion. We have been sliding into one deficit after another through repeated recessions and persistent slack in our economy. A planned cash surplus of $0.6 billion for the fiscal year 1959 became a record cash deficit of $13.1 billion, largely as the result of economic recession.

A planned cash surplus of $1.8 billion for the current fiscal year is turning into a cash deficit of $8.3 billion, largely as the result of economic slack. If we were to slide into recession through failure to act on taxes, the cash deficit for next year would be larger without the tax reduction than the estimated deficit with tax reduction. Indeed, a new recession could break all peace-time deficit records.

And if we were to try to force budget balance by drastic cuts in expenditures - necessarily at the expense of defense and other vital programs - we would not only endanger the security of the country, we would so depress demand, production, and employment that tax revenues would fall and leave the government budget still in deficit.

The attempt would thus be self-defeating. So until we restore full prosperity and the budget balancing revenues it generates, our practical choice is not between deficit and surplus but between two kinds of deficits: between deficits born of waste and weakness and deficits incurred as we build our future strength. If an individual spends frivolously beyond his means today and borrows beyond his prospects for earning tomorrow, this is a sign of weakness.

But if he borrows prudently to invest in a machine that boosts his business profits, or to pay for education and training that boosts his earning power, this can be a source of strength, a deficit through which he builds a better future for himself and his family, a deficit justified by his increased potential. As long as we have large numbers of workers without jobs, and producers without markets, we will as a Nation fall into repeated deficits of inertia and weakness.

But, by comparison, if we enlarge the deficit temporarily as the by-product of our positive tax policy to expand our economy this will serve as a source of strength, not a sign of weakness. It will yield rich private dividends in higher output, faster growth, more jobs, higher profits and incomes; and, by the same token, a large public gain in expanded budget revenues. As the economy returns to full employment, the budget will return to constructive balance. This would not be true, of course, if we were currently straining the limits of our productive capacity, when the dollars released by tax reduction would push against unyielding bottlenecks in industrial plant and skilled manpower.

Then, tax reduction would be an open invitation to inflation, to a renewed price-wage spiral, and would threaten our hard-won balance of payments improvement. Today, however, we not only have unused manpower and idle plant capacity; new additions to the labor force and to plant capacity are constantly enlarging our productive potential. We have an economy fully able and ready to respond to the stimulus of tax reduction.

Our need today, then, is -to provide markets to bring back into production underutilized plant and equipment; -to provide incentives to invest, in the form both of wider markets and larger profits-investment that will expand and modernize, innovate, cut costs; -most important, by means of stronger markets and enlarged investment, to provide jobs for the unemployed and for the new workers streaming into the labor force during the sixties - and, closing the circle, the new jobholders will generate still larger markets and further investment.

It was in direct response to these needs that I pledged last summer to submit proposals for a top-to-bottom reduction in personal and corporate income taxes in 1963 - for reducing the tax burden on private income and the tax deterrents to private initiative that have for too long held economic activity in check. Only when we have removed the heavy drag our fiscal system now exerts on personal and business purchasing power and on the financial incentives for greater risk-taking and personal effort can we expect to restore the high levels of employment and high rate of growth that we took for granted in the first decade after the war.

Taxes and Consumer Demand In order to enlarge markets for consumer goods and services and translate these into new jobs, fuller work schedules, higher profits, and rising farm incomes, I am proposing a major reduction in individual income tax rates. Rates should be cut in three stages, from their present range of 20 to 91 percent to the more reasonable range of 14 to 65 percent.

In the first stage, beginning July 1, these rate reductions will cut individual liabilities at an annual rate of $6 billion. Most of this would translate immediately into greater take-home pay through a reduction in the basic withholding rate. Further rate reductions would apply to 1964 and 1965 incomes, with resulting revenue losses to be partially offset by tax reforms, thus applying a substantial additional boost to consumer markets.

These revisions would directly increase the annual rate of disposable after-tax incomes of American households by about $6 billion in the second half of 1963, and some $8 billion when the program is in full effect, with account taken of both tax reductions and tax reform. Taxpayers in all brackets would benefit, with those in the lower brackets getting the largest proportional reductions. American households as a whole regularly spend between 92 and 94 percent of the total after-tax (disposable) incomes they receive.

And they generally hold to this range even when income rises and falls; so it follows that they generally spend about the same percentage of dollars of income added or subtracted. If we cut about $8 billion from the consumer tax load, we can reasonably expect a direct addition to consumer goods markets of well over $7 billion. A reduction of corporate taxes would provide a further increment to the flow of household incomes as dividends are enlarged; and this, too, would directly swell the consumer spending stream. The direct effects, large as they are, would be only the beginning. Rising output and employment to meet the new demands for consumer goods will generate new income-wages, salaries, and profits. Spending from this extra income flow would create more jobs, more production, and more incomes.

The ultimate increases in the continuing flow of incomes, production, and consumption will greatly exceed the initial amount of tax reduction. Even if the tax program had no influence on investment spending - either directly or indirectly - the $8-9 billion added directly to the flow of consumer income would call forth a flow of at least $16 billion of added consumer goods and services. But the program will also generate direct and indirect increases in investment spending. The production of new machines, and the building of new factories, stores, offices, and apartments add to incomes in the same way as does production of consumer goods. This too sets off a derived chain reaction of consumer spending, adding at least another $1 billion of output of consumer goods for every $1 billion of added investment.

Taxes and Investment To raise the Nation's capacity to produce - to expand the quantity, quality, and variety of our output - we must not merely replace but continually expand, improve, modernize, and rebuild our productive capital. That is, we must invest, and we must grow. The past half decade of unemployment and excess capacity has led to inadequate business investment. In 1962, the rate of investment was almost unchanged from 1957 though gross national product had risen by almost 16 percent, after allowance for price changes. Clearly it is essential to our employment and growth objectives as well as to our international competitive stance that we stimulate more rapid expansion and modernization of America's productive facilities.

FIRST step, we have already provided important new tax incentives for productive investment. Last year the Congress enacted a seven percent tax credit for business expenditures on major kinds of equipment. And the Treasury, at my direction, revised its depreciation rules to reflect today's conditions. Together, these measures are saving business over $2 billion a year in taxes and significantly increasing the net rate of return on capital investments.

SECOND step in my program to lift vestment incentives is to reduce the corporate tax rate from 52 percent to 47 percent, thus restoring the pre-Korean rate. Particularly, to aid small businesses, I am recommending that effective January 1, 1963, the rate on the first $25,000 of corporate income be dropped from 30 to 22 percent while the 52 percent rate on corporate income over $25,000 is retained. In later stages, the 52 percent rate would drop to 47 percent. These changes will cut corporate liabilities by over $2.5 billion before structural changes.

The resulting increase in profitability will encourage risk-taking and enlarge the flow of internal funds which typically finance a major share of corporate investment. In recent periods, business as a whole has not been starved for financial accommodation. But global totals mask the fact that thousands of small or rapidly growing businesses are handicapped by shortage of investible funds. As the total impact of the tax program takes hold and generates pressures on existing capacity, more and more companies will find the lower taxes a welcome source of finance for plant expansion.

THIRD step toward higher levels of capital spending is a combination of structural changes to remove barriers to the full flow of investment funds, to sharpen the incentives for creative investment, and to remove tax-induced distortions in resource flow. Reduction of the top individual income tax rate from 91 to 65 percent is a central part of this balanced program.

FOURTH, apart from direct measures to courage investment, the tax program will go to the heart of the main deterrent to investment today, namely, inadequate markets. Once the sovereign incentive of high and rising sales is restored, and the businessman is convinced that today's new plant and equipment will find profitable use tomorrow, the effects of the directly stimulative measures will be doubled and redoubled. Thus - and it is no contradiction - the most important single thing we can do to stimulate investment in today's economy is to raise consumption by major reduction of individual income tax rates.

FIFTH, side-by-side with tax measures, I am confident that the Federal Reserve and the Treasury will continue to maintain, consistent with their responsibilities for the external defense of the dollar, monetary and credit conditions favorable to the flow of savings into long-term investment in the productive strength of the country. Given a series of large and timely tax reductions and reforms, as I have proposed, we can surely achieve the balanced expansion of consumption and investment so urgently needed to overcome a half decade of slack and to capitalize on the great and growing economic opportunities of the decade ahead.

The impact of my tax proposals on the budget deficit will be cushioned by the scheduling of reductions in several stages rather than a single large cut; the careful pruning of civilian expenditures for fiscal 1964 - those other than for defense, space, and debt service-to levels below fiscal 1963; the adoption of a more current time schedule for tax payments of large corporations, which will at the outset add about $1 1/2 billion a year to budget receipts; the net offset of $3 1/2 billion of revenue loss by selected structural changes in the income tax; most powerfully, in time, by the accelerated growth of taxable income and tax receipts as the economy expands in response to the stimulus of the tax program. Impact on the Debt Given the deficit now in prospect, action to raise the existing legal limit on the public debt will be required.

The ability of the Nation to service the Federal debt rests on the income of its citizens whose taxes must pay the interest. Total Federal interest payments as a fraction of the national income have fallen, from eight percent in 1946 to 2.1 percent last year. The gross debt itself as a proportion of our GNP has also fallen steadily - from 123 percent in 1946 to 55 percent last year. Under the budgetary changes scheduled this year and next, these ratios will continue their decline.

It is also of interest to compare the rise in Federal debt with the rise in other forms of debt. Since the end of 1946, the Federal debt held by the public has risen by billion; net State/local debt, by $58 billion; net corporate debt, by $237 billion; and net total private debt, by $518 billion. Clearly, we would prefer smaller debts than we have today. But this does not settle the issue. The central requirement is that debt be incurred only for constructive purposes and at times and in ways that serve to strengthen the position of the debtor. In the case of the Federal Government, where the Nation is the debtor, the key test is whether the increase serves to strengthen or weaken our economy.

In terms of jobs and output generated without threat to price stability - and in terms of the resulting higher revenue - the debt increases foreseen under my tax program clearly pass this test. Monetary and debt management policies can accommodate our debt increase in 1963 - as they did in 1961 and 1962 - without inflationary strain or restriction of private credit availability.

TAX REDUCTION & FISCAL POLICY

While the basic purpose of my tax program is to meet our longer run economic challenges, we should not forget its role in strengthening our defenses against recession. Enactment on schedule of this program which involves a total of over $10 billion of net income tax reduction annually would be a major counterforce to any recessionary tendencies that might appear. Nevertheless, when our calendar of fiscal legislation is lighter than it is in 1963, it will be important to erect further defenses against recession.

Last year, I proposed that the Congress provide the President with limited standby authority (1) to initiate, subject to Congressional veto, temporary reductions in individual income tax rates and (2) to accelerate and initiate properly timed public capital improvements in times of serious and rising unemployment. Work on the development of an acceptable plan for quick tax action to counter future recessions should continue; with the close cooperation of the Congress, it should be possible to combine provision for swift action with full recognition of the Constitutional role of the Congress in taxation.

TAX REVISION.

Their report urges the central significance of prompt tax reduction and reform in a program for economic growth: first, for the sustained lift it will give to the economy's demand for goods and services, and thus to the expansion of its productive capacity; second, for the added incentive to productive investment, risk-taking, and efficient use of resources that will come from lowering the corporate tax rate and the unrealistic top rates on personal income, and eliminating unwarranted tax preferences that undermine the tax base and misdirect energy and resources. I have already laid the case for major tax changes before you, and I will submit detailed legislation and further analysis in a special message.

I remind you now that my 1963 tax proposals are central to a program to tilt the trend of American growth upward and to achieve our share of the 50-percent growth target which was adopted for the decade of the sixties by the 20 member nations of the Organization for Economic Cooperation and Development.

POLICIES FOR FASTER GROWTH.

The tax program I have outlined is phased over 3 years. Its invigorating effects will be felt far longer. For among the costs of prolonged slack is slow growth. An economy that fails to use its productive potential fully feels no need to increase it rapidly. The incentive to invest is bent beneath the weight of excess capacity. Lack of employment opportunities slows the growth of the labor force. Defensive restrictive practices - from featherbedding to market sharing - flourish when limited markets, jobs, and incentives shrink the scope for effort and ingenuity.

But when the economy breaks out of the lethargy of the past 5 or 6 years, the end to economic slack will by itself mean faster growth. Full employment will relax the grip of restrictive practices and open the gates wider to innovation and change. Tax reduction will remove an obstacle to the full development of the forces of growth in a free economy.

To go further, public policy must offer positive support to the primary sources of economic energy. I propose that the Federal Government lay the groundwork now for positive action in three key areas, each singled out by the Cabinet Committee as fundamental to the long-run strength and resilience of our economy: (1) the stimulation of civilian technology, (2) the support of education, and (3) the development of manpower.

In each of these areas I shall make specific proposals for action. Together with tax revision, they mark the beginning of a more conscious and active policy for economic growth. Support of industry research associations - Adjustment of the income tax laws to give business firms an additional stimulus to invest in research equipment.[78]

JOHN F. KENNEDY, JANUARY 24, 1963, MESSAGE TO CONGRESS ON TAX REDUCTION AND REFORM:

The most urgent task facing our Nation at home today is to end the tragic waste of unemployment and unused resources - to step up the growth and vigor of our national economy - to increase job and investment opportunities - to improve our productivity - and thereby to strengthen our nation's ability to meet its world-wide commitments for the defense and growth of freedom.

The revision of our Federal tax system on an equitable basis is crucial to the achievement of these goals. Originally designed to hold back war and postwar inflation, our present income tax rate structure now holds back consumer demand, initiative, and investment. After the war and during the Korean conflict, the outburst of civilian demand and inflation justified the retention of this level and structure of rates.

But it has become increasingly dear-particularly in the last five years-that the largest single barrier to full employment of our manpower and resources and to a higher rate of economic growth is the unrealistically heavy drag of Federal income taxes on private purchasing power, initiative and incentive. Our economy is checkreined today by a war-born tax system at a time when it is far more in need of the spur than the bit.

My recommendation for early revision of our tax structure is not motivated by any threat of imminent recession - nor should it be rejected by any fear of inflation or of weakening the dollar as a world currency. The chief problem confronting our economy in 1963 is its unrealized potential - slow growth, under-investment, unused capacity and persistent unemployment. The result is lagging wage, salary and profit income, smaller take-home pay, insufficient productivity gains, inadequate Federal revenues and persistent Budget deficits.

One recession has followed another, with each period of recovery and expansion fading out earlier than the last. Our gains fall far short of what we could do and need to do, measured both in terms of our past record and the accomplishments of our overseas competitors.

Despite the improvements resulting from last year's depreciation reform and investment credit - which I pledged two years ago would be only a first step-our tax system still siphons out of the private economy too large a share of personal and business purchasing power and reduces the incentive for risk, investment and effort - thereby aborting our recoveries and stifling our national growth rate.

In addition, the present tax code contains special preferences and provisions, all of which narrow the tax base (thus requiring higher rates), artificially distort the use of resources, inhibit the mobility and formation of capital, add complexities and inequities which undermine the morale of the taxpayer, and make tax avoidance rather than market factors a prime consideration in too many economic decisions.

I am therefore proposing the following:

(1) Reduction in individual income tax rates from their present levels of 20 to 91 percent, to a range of 14 to 65 percent-the 14 percent rate to apply to the first $2,000 of taxable income for married taxpayers filing joint returns, and to the first $1,000 of the taxable income of single taxpayers;

(2) Reduction in the rate of the corporate income tax from 52 to 47 percent;

(3) Reversal of the corporate normal and surtax rates, so that the tax rate applicable to the first $25,000 of corporate income would drop from 30 to 22 percent, so as to give particular encouragement to small business;

(4) Acceleration of tax payments by corporations with anticipated annual liabilities of more than $100,000, to bring the corporate payment schedule to a current basis over a five year transition period;

(5) Revision of the tax treatment of capital gains, designed to provide a freer and fuller flow of capital funds and to achieve a greater equity;

(6) Removal of certain inequities and hardships in our present tax structure; and

(7) Broadening of the base of the individual and corporate income taxes, to remove unwarranted special privileges, correct defects in the tax law, and provide more equal treatment of taxpayers - thereby permitting a larger reduction in tax rates than would otherwise be possible and making possible my proposals to alleviate hardships and inequities. The tax program I am recommending for enactment in 1963

would become fully effective by January, 1965. The rate reductions provide a cut in tax liabilities of $13.6 billion - $11 billion for individuals and $2.6 billion for corporations.

Other adjustments, some of which lose and some of which gain revenue, would, on balance, produce a revenue gain of $3-4 billion, leaving a net reduction of $10.2 billion. Accelerating tax payments of large corporations to a correct basis over a five-year transition period would reduce the effect on tax receipts to $8.7 billion. These figures do not include off-setting revenue gains which would result from the stimulating effects of the program on the economy as a whole and on the level of taxable income, profits and sales - gains which may be expected to increase as the economy recaptures its vigor, and to lead to higher total tax receipts than would otherwise be realized.

I. BENEFITS TO THE ECONOMY.

Enactment of this program will help strengthen every segment of the American economy and bring us closer to every basic objective of American economic policy. -Total output and economic growth will be stepped up by an amount several times as great as the tax cut itself. Total incomes will rise - billions of dollars more will be earned each year in profits and wages. Investment and productivity improvement will be spurred by more intensive use of our present productive potential; and the added incentives to risk-taking will speed the modernization of American industry.

Additional dollars spent by consumers or invested by producers will lead to more jobs, more plant capacity, more markets and thus still more dollars for consumption and investment. Idle manpower and plant capacity make this possible without inflation; and strong and healthy economic activity is the best insurance against future recessions. -Unemployment will be reduced, as firms throughout the country hire new workers to meet the new demands released by tax reduction.

The economic prospects of our depressed areas will improve as investors obtain new incentives to create additional productive facilities in areas of labor surplus. Pressure for the 35-hour week, for new import barriers or for other shortsighted and restrictive measures will be lessened. Companies and workers will find it easier to adjust to import competition.

Low income farmers will be drawn to new jobs which offer a better livelihood. The retraining of workers with obsolete skills will proceed more quickly and efficiently in a full employment climate. Those presently employed will have greater job security and increased assurance of a full work week. -Price stability can be maintained. Inflationary forces need not be revived by strengthening the economy at a time of substantial unemployment and unused capacity with a properly constructed program of tax reduction.

With the gains in disposable income of wage earners there should be less pressure for wage increases in excess of gains in productivity - and with increased profits after tax there should be less pressure to raise prices. Inflationary expectations have ended; monetary tools are working well; and the increasing productivity and modernization resulting from new levels of investment will facilitate a reduction of costs and the maintenance of price stability. This nation is growing - its needs are growing - and tax revision now will steadily increase our capacity to meet those needs at a time when there are no major bottlenecks in manpower, plant or resources, no emergencies straining our reserves of productive power, and no lack of vigorous competition from other nations.

Nor need anyone fear that the deficit will be financed in an inflationary manner. The balanced approach that the Treasury has followed in its management of the public debt can be relied upon to prevent any inflationary push. -Our balance of payments should be improved by the fiscal policies reflected in this program. Its enactment - which will make investment in America more profitable, ,and which will increase the efficiency of American plants, thus cutting costs and improving our competitive position in world trade-will provide the strongest possible economic backing for the dollar. Lagging growth contributes to a lack of confidence in the dollar, and the movement of capital abroad. Accelerated growth will attract capital to these shores and bolster our free world leadership in terms of both our strength and our example.

Moreover, a nation operating closer to capacity will be freer to use monetary tools to protect its international accounts, should events so require. -Consumers will convert a major percentage of their personal income tax savings into a higher standard of living, benefiting their own families while generating stronger markets for producers. Even modest increases in take-home pay enable consumers to undertake larger periodic payments on major purchases, as well as to increase purchases of smaller items - and either type of purchase leads to further income and employment. -Investment will be expanded, as the rate of return on capital formation is increased, and as growing consumer markets create a need for new capacity.

It is no contradiction to say that the best means of increasing investment today is to increase consumption and market demand - and reductions in individual tax rates will do this. In addition, reducing the corporate tax from 52% to 47% will mean not only greater incentives to invest but more internal funds available for investment. Reducing the maximum individual income tax rate from 91% to 65% makes more meaningful the concept of additional reward and incentive for additional initiative, effort and risk-taking. A rising level of consumer demand will enable the more than $2 billion worth of investment incentives provided by last year's tax actions (the depreciation reform and investment credit) to achieve their full effect. In addition, tax reform will reduce those distortions of effort which interfere with a more efficient allocation of investment funds.

The cumulative effect of this additional investment is once again more income, therefore more consumer demand, and therefore still more investment. -State and local governments, hard pressed by a considerably faster rise in expenditures and indebtedness than that experienced at the Federal level, will also gain additional revenues without increasing their own tax rates as national income and production expand.

II. BENEFITS TO THE TAXPAYER.

The increased purchasing power and strengthened incentives which will move us toward our national goals will reach to all corners of our population and to all segments of our business community. - Wage-earners and low-income families will gain an immediate increase in take-home pay as soon as the tax program is enacted and new withholding rates go into effect.

While tax rates are to be reduced for every bracket, the largest proportionate tax reduction properly goes to those at the bottom of the economic ladder. Accordingly, in addition to lowering rates in the lower brackets, I urge that the first bracket be split into two groups, so that married couples with 'adjusted gross incomes' of $2,000 or less (or single persons with $1,000 or less) receive a 30% reduction in their tax rate. Some one-third of all taxpayers are in this group- including many of the very old and very young whose earning powers are below average.

Many of the structural revisions proposed below are also designed to meet hardships which rate reduction alone will not alleviate- hardships to low-income families and individuals, to older workers and to working mothers. This program is far preferable to an increase in exemptions, because, with a far smaller loss of revenue, it focuses the gains far more sharply on those who need it most and will spend it quickly, with benefits to the entire economy. -Middle and higher-income families are both consumers and investors - and the present rates ranging up to 91% not only check consumption but discourage investment, and encourage the diversion of funds and effort into activities aimed more at the avoidance of taxes than the efficient production of goods.

The oppressive impact of those high rates gave rise to many of the undue preferences in the present law - and both the high rates and the preferences should be ended in the new law. Under present conditions, the highest rate should not exceed 65%, a reduction of 29% from the present rate-accompanied by appropriate reductions in the middle income ranges.

This will restore an idea that has helped make our country great-that a person who devotes his efforts to increasing his income, thereby adding to the nation's income and wealth, should be able to retain a reasonable share of the results. - Businessmen and farmers - everyone whose income depends directly upon selling his products or services to the public - will benefit from the increased income and purchasing power of consumers and the substantial reduction in taxes on profits.

The attainment of full employment and full capacity is even

more important to profits than the reduction in corporate taxes; for, even in the absence of such reduction, profits after taxes would be at least 15% higher today if we were operating at full employment. Enactment of a program aimed at helping reach full employment and capacity use which also reduces the Government's interest in corporate profits to 47% instead of 52%, thus lowering corporate tax liabilities by a further $2.6 billion a year - while increasing consumer demand by some $8 billion a year - will surely give American industry new incentive to expand production and capacity. -Small businessmen with net income of less than $25,000 - who constitute over 450,000 of the Nation's 585,000 corporations will, under this program, receive greater reductions in their corporation taxes than their larger competitors.

Under my program, beginning this year, the first $25,000 of corporate taxable income will be subject to a tax rate of 22 percent rather than 30 percent, a reduction of almost 27%. This change is important to those small corporations which have less ready access to the capital markets, must depend more heavily for capital on internally generated funds, and are generally at a financial and competitive disadvantage. Unincorporated businesses, of course, will benefit from the reduction in individual income taxes.

III. THE TAX PROGRAM AND THE FEDERAL BUDGET.

A balanced Federal budget in a growing full employment economy will be most rapidly and certainly achieved by a substantial expansion in national income carrying with it the needed Federal revenues - the kind of expansion the proposed tax revision is designed to bring about. Within a few years of the enactment of this program, Federal revenues will be larger than if present tax rates continue to prevail.

Full employment, moreover, will make possible the reduction of certain Government expenditures caused by unemployment. As the economy climbs toward full employment, a substantial part of the increased tax revenue thereby generated will be applied toward a reduction in the Federal deficit.

As I have repeatedly emphasized, our choice today is not between a tax cut and a balanced budget. Our choice is between chronic deficits resulting from chronic slack, on the one hand, and transitional deficits temporarily enlarged by tax revision designed to promote full employment and thus make possible an ultimately balanced budget. Because this chronic slack produces inadequate revenues, the projected administrative deficit for fiscal 1964 - without any tax reduction, leaving the present system intact - would be 19.2 billion.

The inclusion of the tax program - after the 'feed-back' in revenues from its economic stimulus and the acceleration of corporate tax payments - will add only an additional $2.7 billion loss in receipts, bringing the projected deficit in the administrative budget to $11.9 billion. The issue now is whether the strengthening of our economy which will result from the tax program is worth an addition of $2.7 billion to the 1964 deficit. If the tax brake on our economy is not released, the slack will remain, Federal revenues will lag and budget deficits will persist.

In fact, another recession would produce a record peace-time deficit that would far exceed $11.9 billion, and without the positive effects of tax reduction. But once this tax brake is released, the base of taxable income, wages, and profits will grow - and a temporary increase in the deficit will turn into a permanent increase in Federal revenues. The purpose of cutting taxes, I repeat, is not to create a deficit but to increase investment, employment and the prospects for a balanced budget. It would be a grave mistake to require that any tax reduction today be offset by a corresponding cut in expenditures. In my judgment,

I have proposed the minimum level of Federal expenditures needed for the security of the Nation, for meeting the challenge facing us in space, and for the well being of our people. Moreover, the gains in demand from tax reduction would then be offset - or more than offset - by the loss of demand due to the reduction in Government spending. The incentive effects of tax reduction would remain, but total jobs and output would shrink as Government contracts were cut back, workers were laid off and projects were ended. On the other hand, I do not favor raising demand by a massive increase in Government expenditures. In today's circumstances, it is desirable to seek expansion through our free market processes - to place increased spending power in the hands of private consumers and investors and offer more encouragement to private initiative.

The most effective policy, therefore, is to expand demand and unleash incentives through a program of tax reduction and reform, coupled with the most prudent possible policy of public expenditures. To carry out such a policy, the fiscal 1964 budget reduces total outlays other than defense, space and interest charges below their present levels-despite the fact that such expenditures have risen at an average rate of 7.5 percent during the last nine years.

Federal civilian employment under this budget provides for the same number of people to serve every 100 persons in our population as was true when this Administration took office, a smaller ratio than prevailed 10 years ago. The public debt as a proportion of our gross national product will fall to 53%, compared to 57% when this Administration took office. Last year the total increase in the federal debt was only 2 per cent - compared to an 8 per cent increase in the gross debt of state and local governments. Taking a longer view, the federal debt today is only 13 per cent higher than it was in 1946-while state and local debt increased over 360 per cent and private debt by 300 per cent. In fact, if it were not for federal financial assistance to state and local governments, the federal cast: budget would actually show a surplus.

Federal civilian employment, for example, is actually lower today than it was in 1952, while state and local government employment over the same period has increased 67 percent. This Administration is pledged to enforce, economy and efficiency in a strict control of expenditures. In short, this tax program will increase our wealth far more than it increases our public debt. The actual burden of that debt - as measured in relation to our total output-will decline. To continue to increase our debt as the result of inadequate earnings is a sign of weakness. But to borrow prudently in order to invest in a tax revision that will greatly increase our earning power can be a source of strength.

IV. REQUIREMENTS FOR EFFECTIVE ACTION AND FISCAL RESPONSIBILITY.

Fully recognizing that it is both desirable and necessary for the Congress to exercise its own discretion in the actual drafting of a tax bill, I recommend the application of the following basic principles in this vital task:

A. The entire tax revision program should be promptly enacted as a single comprehensive bill. The sooner the program is enacted, the sooner it will make its impact upon the economy, providing additional benefits and further insurance against recession. While the full rate reduction program must take effect gradually for the reasons stated below, I am proposing that the individual tax rates for 1963 income be reduced to a range from 18.5 percent to 84.5 percent, with a cut in the withholding rate from the present 18 percent to 15.5 percent becoming effective upon enactment of the law. This will increase the disposable income of consumers at an annual rate of nearly $6 billion a year in the second half of 1963.

Also the rate of corporate tax on the first $25,000 of net income would be reduced from 30 percent to 22 percent for the year 1963. Equally important is action in 1963 on the additional individual and corporate rate reductions proposed for 1964 and 1965. The prompt enactment of a bill assuring this combination of realized and prospective tax reductions will improve the business climate and public psychology, induce forward business planning, and increase individual incentives. It will enable investors and producers to act this year on the basis of solid expectations of increased market demand and a higher rate of return. To delay decisive action beyond 1963 risks the loss of opportunity and initiative which this year uniquely offers.

B. The net amount of tax reduction enacted should keep within the limits of economic sufficiency and fiscal responsibility. Too small a tax cut would be a waste, gaining us little but further deficits. It could not cope with the task of closing a $30 to $40 billion gap in our economic performance. But the net tax cut of over $10 billion envisioned by this program can lead the way to strong economic expansion and a larger revenue yield. On the other hand, responsible fiscal policy requires that we avoid an overly sharp drop in budgetary receipts for fiscal 1964-65, and that we hold the temporary increase in the deficit below the level which in the past has proved both manageable and compatible with price stability. Therefore, to make these reductions possible, I propose a program:

(a) to phase the tax reductions over a three year period, with the final step effective January 1, 1965;

(b) to couple these reductions, amounting to $13.6 billion, with selected structural changes and reforms gaining $3.4 billion net in revenues; and

(c) to offset the revenue loss still further, during the next five years by gradually moving the tax payments of larger corporations to a more current time schedule, without any change in their tax liabilities.

C. Tax reduction and structural reform should be considered and enacted as a single integrated program. My recommendations for rate reductions of $13.6 billion are made in the expectation that selected structural changes and reforms will be adopted, adding on balance $3.4 billion in revenue and resulting in a net reduction in tax liabilities of no more than $10.2 billion. Larger cuts would create a larger budget deficit and the possibility of renewed inflationary pressures.

Therefore, should the Congress make any significant reductions in the revenues to be raised by structural changes, these reductions would have to be offset by substantially equivalent increases in revenue; and this could only be achieved by sacrificing either some of the important rate reductions I have proposed or some of the measures I am recommending to relieve hardship and promote growth. On the other hand, an attempt to solve all tax problems at once by the inclusion of even more sweeping reforms might impair the effect of rate reduction. This program is designed to achieve broad acceptance and prompt enactment. Some reforms will improve the tax structure by reducing certain liabilities.

Others will broaden the tax base by raising liabilities, and will meet with resistance from those who benefit from existing preferences. But if this program of tax reduction is aimed at making the most of our economic potential, it should be remembered that these preferences and special provisions also restrict our rate of growth and distort the flow of investment. They discourage taxpayer cooperation and compliance by adding inequities and complexities that affect similarly situated taxpayers in wholly different ways. They divert energies from productive activities to tax avoidance - and from more valuable or efficient undertakings to less valuable undertakings with lower tax consequences.

Some departures from uniform tax treatment are required to promote overriding national objectives. But taxpayers with equal incomes who are burdened with unequal tax liabilities are certain to seek still further preferences and exceptions - and to use their resources where they yield the greatest returns after tax even though producing less before taxes, thus lowering our national output and efficiency. Tax reduction is urgently needed to spur the growth of our economy - but both the fruits of growth and the burdens of the resulting new tax structure should be fairly shared by all. For the present patchwork of special provisions lightens the load on some by placing a heavier burden on others.

Because they reduce the tax base, they compel a higher tax rate-and the reduction in the top rate from 91% to 65%, which in itself is a major reform, cannot be justified if these other forms of preferential tax treatment remain. The resistance to tax reform should be less when it is coupled with more-than-offsetting tax reductions benefiting all brackets - and the support for tax reform should be greater when it is a necessary condition for greater tax reduction.

Reform, as mentioned earlier, includes top-to-bottom rate reduction as well as structural change-and the two are inseparable prerequisites to the achievement of our economic and equity objectives. The new rates should be both lower and more widely applicable - for the excessively high rates and various tax concessions have in the past been associated with each other, and they should be eliminated together.

In short, these changes in our tax structure are as essential to maximizing our growth and use of resources as rate reduction, and make a greater rate reduction possible. The broader the Congress can extend the tax base, the lower it can reduce the tax rates. But to the extent that the erosion of our tax base by special preferences is not reversed to gain some $3.4 billion net, Congress will have to forgo - for reasons of both equity and fiscal responsibility-either corporate or personal rate reductions now contained in the program.

V. PROPOSALS FOR RATE REDUCTION.

The central thrust of this proposed tax program is contained in the most thorough overhaul in tax rates in more than 20 substantially reducing rates at all levels, for both individuals and corporations, by a total of $13.6 billion. While the principal components of my proposals for rate reduction have been alluded to in the foregoing discussion, it might be well to specify them in detail here. Reduction in individual income tax rates.

Personal tax liabilities will creased by $11 billion through a reduction in rates from their present levels of 20-25% to a range of 14-65%, with appropriate reductions generally averaging more than and covering every bracket. The lowest 14% rate would apply to the first $2,,000 taxable income for married taxpayers filing joint returns, and to the first $1,000 of the taxable income of single taxpayers - a reduction of 30% in the taxes levied on this new bracket, in which falls the entire taxable income of 1/3 of all taxpayers.

The new maximum rate of 65% would enable those individuals who now keep only 9 cents out of each additional dollar earned to retain 35 cents in the future. I am attaching tables showing the proposed rate schedules for married and single taxpayers. These reductions would take place over a 3-year period:

-For calendar year 1963, I propose a rate schedule ranging from 18.5% to 84.5%, reducing the appropriate withholding rate immediately upon enactment from its present level of 18% to a new level of 15.5%.

-For purposes of taxpayer computations, the new tax rates would apply to the entire calendar year, thus requiring the lower withholding rate to minimize over-withholding.

-For calendar year 1964, I propose a rate schedule ranging from 15.5% to 71.5%, effective for the entire year and accompanied by a withholding rate of 13.5% beginning July 1 of that year.

-For calendar year 1965 and thereafter, I propose a permanent rate schedule ranging from 14 to 65%, maintaining the withholding rate at 13.5%. Reductions in the corporate income tax rate will cut corporate tax liabilities by $2.6 billion per year (in addition to the reduction of $2 billion per year provided by the 1962 investment tax credit and depreciation reform), and take effect in three stages:

-For calendar year 1963, the present normal tax of 30%,

applicable to the first $25,000 of taxable corporate income (the entire earnings of almost half a million small corporations) would drop to 22%, a reduction of almost 27%, while the rate applicable to income in excess of $25,000 would remain at 52%, thus reversing the present normal tax of 30% and the surtax of 22%. The normal tax would remain permanently at 22%.

-For calendar year 1964, the corporate surtax would be reduced to 28%, thereby lowering the combined corporate rate to 50%.

-For calendar year 1965 and thereafter, the corporate surtax would be reduced to 25%, thereby lowering the combined corporate rate to 47% and ending the role of the Government as a senior partner in business profits. Since the $25,000 surtax exemption and the new 22% normal rate are designed to stimulate small business, this reduction should be accompanied by action designed to eliminate the advantage of the multiple surtax exemptions now available to large enterprises operating through a chain of separately incorporated units. I, therefore, recommend that legislation be enacted which, over a transitional period of 5 years, will limit to one the number of surtax exemptions allowed an affiliated corporate group subject to 80 percent common control.

This proposal would apply both to affiliated groups having a common corporate parent and to enterprises sharing common individual ownership. It will add $120 million annually to tax receipts. On the other hand, if affiliated corporations are treated as an entity for the surtax exemption and other purposes, they should be permitted to obtain the advantages of filing consolidated returns without incurring the present tax of 2% on the net income of all corporations filing such returns. The a percent tax was removed in 1954 from consolidated returns of regulated public utility enterprises; and I recommend that it be repealed for all corporate enterprises beginning in 1964. This proposal will contribute to a more realistic corporate tax rate structure and reduce the adverse effect of high marginal tax rates on growth-at an annual cost to the Treasury of only $50 million. To offset revenue losses by an estimated $1.5 billion per year over the next five years, without increasing the actual net burden of tax liability of corporations, I recommend that corporations with an annual tax liability in excess of

$100,000 - which are now on a partially current payment basis - be placed on a more current tax payment schedule beginning in 1964.

Under this plan, such corporations would make a first declaration and payment of estimated tax on April 15, with subsequent payments due on June 15, September 15 and December 15, reaching a fully current basis similar to that required of individual income taxpayers after a 5 year transition period. More current payment of corporate taxes will strengthen the Government's budgetary position, but will not - even during the five-year transition period - offset the benefits of rate reduction for these corporations.

VI. PROPOSALS FOR STRUCTURAL REVISION & REFORM.

The changes listed below are an integral part of a single tax package which should be enacted this year. All of them should be effective January 1, 1964. Some remove inequities and hardships and thus further reduce revenues; others recoup revenue by revising preferential tax treatment now accorded particular types of transactions, enterprises or taxpayers. Their combined revenue effect makes possible $3.4 billion of the $13.6 billion reduction in tax rates, for a net reduction of $10.2 billion.

But their combined economic effect is even more important to provide greater equity in a broader tax base, to encourage the full and efficient flow of capital, to remove unwarranted special privileges and hardships, to simplify tax administration and compliance and to release for more productive endeavors the energies now devoted to avoiding taxes.

While rate reductions are also a major reform, they are in large part justified and weakened by the absence of substantial rate made possible by structural reform - and the case for structural reform, in turn, would be reduction. These reforms may be divided into three categories:

A) Relief of hardship and encouragement of growth;

B) Base broadening and equity; and

C) Revision of capital gains taxation for growth and equity.

(A) Relief of Hardship & Encouragement of Growth

1. A minimum standard deduction. I do not believe that the

individual income tax should apply at levels of income as low as $667 for single persons and $1,333 for married couples as it does now. One way to provide relief to low income taxpayers - in addition to the splitting of the first bracket as already recommended - would be to raise the personal exemption above its present level of $600. This is an extremely costly approach, however, and one which would not fulfill our objective of giving relief where it is needed most.

As a more effective and less costly means of securing the same objective, I recommend the adoption of a minimum standard deduction of $300 ($150 for each spouse filing a separate return) plus $100 per dependent up to the present maximum of $1,000. Under present law the standard deduction cannot exceed 10 percent of a person's income.

The establishment of a minimum standard deduction will provide about $220 million of tax relief, primarily to those with income below $5,000. If this proposal is adopted, single individuals would remain free of income tax liability until their incomes exceeded 1900 rather than the present $667, thus giving them the equivalent of an increase in the personal exemption of $233. A married couple, without dependents, now subject to tax on income in excess of $1,333, would be taxed only on income in excess of $1,500.

A couple with two dependents would be taxed only on income in excess of $2,900, as compared with $2,667 under present law. A more liberal child care deduction. Employed women, widowers, and divorced men are now allowed a deduction of up to $600 per year for expenses incurred for the care of children and other dependents who are unable to care for themselves. In its present form this provision fails far short of fulfilling its objective of providing tax relief to those who must in order to work - meet extra expenses for the care of dependents. I recommend increasing the maximum amount that may be deducted from the present $600 to $1,000 where three or more children must be cared for. I also recommend three further steps: raising from $4,500 to $7,000 the amount of income that families with working wives can have and still remain fully eligible; increasing the age limit of children who qualify from 11 to 12; and extending the deduction to certain taxpayers who now do not qualify-such as a married man whose wife is confined to an institution.

The revenue cost of these changes in the child care deduction would be $20 million per year, most of which would benefit taxpayers with incomes of less than $7,000. The tax treatment of older people. The special problems encountered by older people are recognized in a variety of not always consistent provisions under the present individual income tax law, resulting in widely different tax burdens for similarly situated older people whose incomes are derived from different sources.

The relief is not only unevenly distributed, but, to the extent that its benefits accrue to those with high income, is unnecessary, wasting revenue which could be used to provide more adequately for those who need it. For example: a single taxpayer aged 65, whose income of $5,000 is entirely in the form of wages, now pays an income tax of $686. If he were retired and his income were in the form of dividends, his tax liability would be less than half as much - $329. Moreover, the extra $600 exemption helps most those with substantial incomes. I am convinced, therefore, that a more uniform and equitable approach, one which will reduce and tend to equalize the tax burdens of all lower and modest income older people, is required.

To this end, I recommend that all people aged 65 or over, regardless of the source of their income, be allowed a credit of $300 against taxes otherwise owing. This credit would replace both the extra exemption allowed to older people and the retirement income credit, and would be of far greater value to the vast majority of older taxpayers. Under present law the amount of retirement income utilized in computing the retirement income credit is reduced, dollar for dollar, by social security and railroad retirement benefits received.

The proposed $300 credit would also be reduced but only by a limited amount. (This amount would be equal to the taxpayer's bracket rate times one-half of the benefits - that portion attributable to the employer's contribution.) This treatment of social security and railroad retirement benefits is more favorable than .present law in its effect on lower and middle income taxpayers; and, indeed, the overall result of this proposal for a $300 credit would be to liberalize substantially the tax treatment of aged lower and middle income taxpayers.

Although this provision would moderately reduce the benefits of aged upper income taxpayers, they stand to gain substantially from the general rate reduction and will still pay lower taxes. Those whose incomes are wholly or primarily in the form of social security or railroad retirement benefits, of course, will still not be subject to income tax and these benefits will remain excludable from income. The enactment of this recommendation will ensure that single older people will not be subject to individual income tax liability unless their incomes exceed $2,900 (for married couples $5,800). These figures contrast with as little as $1,333 for single older individuals and $2,667 for older married couples under present law.

It will also remove the existing excessively high tax cost imposed upon those older people who, out of preference or necessity, continue in gainful employment. The vital skills and energies of these older workers should not be discouraged from contributing materially to our economic strength. A further major advantage of this recommendation is that it will greatly simplify the filing of tax returns for our older people. As much as two-thirds of a page of the individual income tax return now required for computation of the retirement income credit will be eliminated. In addition, a large number of older people who presently file tax returns will no longer find it necessary to do so because the filing requirement will be raised from $1,200 to $1,800.

The revenue reduction associated with these gains in equity and simplicity in the tax treatment of older people will be $320 million per year. Income averaging. Many taxpayers are heavily penalized if they receive income in widely fluctuating amounts from year to year. I have instructed the Secretary of the Treasury to present to the Congress as part of this program an income averaging provision. It will provide fairer tax treatment for those who receive in a single taxable year unusually large amounts of income as compared to their average income for preceding years. This proposal will go beyond the narrowly confined and complex averaging provisions of present law and will permit their elimination from the Internal Revenue Code. It will provide one formula of general application to those with wide fluctuations in income.

This means fairer tax treatment for authors, professional artists, actors and athletes, as well as farmers, ranchers, fishermen, attorneys, architects and others. The estimated annual revenue cost of this proposal is $30 million. Employees - moving expenses. Under present law employees are allowed to exclude from their taxable income any reimbursement received from their employer for moving expenses when changing their place of residence and job location while continuing to work for the same employer. In order to facilitate labor mobility and provide more equal treatment of similarly situated taxpayers, I recommend appropriate extension of this tax benefit to new employees.

This recommendation will entail a revenue loss of $20 million per year. Charitable contributions. Under present law an extra 10 percent deduction over and above the basic 20 percent limitation on deductions for charitable contributions is allowable for contributions to churches, educational institutions, and medical facilities and research. I recommend that this limit on the deduction for charitable contributions be liberalized and made more uniform.

To this end the 30 percent limit should extend to all organizations eligible for the charitable contributions deduction which are publicly supported and controlled. This recommendation can be implemented at a revenue cost which is minor. But it will prove advantageous to the advancement of highly desirable activities in our communities, such as symphony orchestras and the work of community chests and cultural centers. Research and Development. Current business expenses for research and experimental purposes may now be deducted as incurred. But under present law the cost of machinery and equipment, now so vital to modern research and development activities, must be capitalized and the cost deducted only over the useful life of the machinery or equipment.

As a spur to private research and development, so essential to the growth of our economy, I recommend that expenditures for machinery and equipment used directly in research or development activities be allowed as a current expense deduction. I am confident that this measure, which will involve a revenue cost of some $50 million, will provide future benefits in the form of better products, lower costs, and larger markets. These benefits, in turn, will bear: fruit in larger tax bases and budgetary receipts.

(B) Base Broadening and Equity. A floor under itemized deductions of individuals. Most taxpayers use the 'standard deduction', generally equal to 10 percent of income up to a maximum of $1,000. But ever since this standard deduction was introduced during World War II, the proportion of taxpayers using it has declined steadily. At present, more than 40 percent of all individual income tax returns are filed by people who itemize deductions for a variety of deductible personal expenses, such as State and local taxes, interest, charitable contributions, medical expenses and casualty losses. The amount of itemized deductions claimed on tax returns has gone up sharply-from less than $6 billion in 1942 to $25.7 in 1957 and $40 billion in 1962.

The present practice of allowing taxpayers to deduct certain expenses in full-the only exception being medical expenses which are subject to a three-percent floor plus a x percent floor for drugs - raises difficult problems of equity, taxpayer compliance, and tax administration and enforcement. One purpose of itemized deductions is to relieve those taxpayers who are burdened by certain expenses or hardships in unusually large amounts, such as those involved in heavy casualty losses or serious illness.

Another purpose is to stimulate certain desirable activities, such as charitable contributions or home ownership. Where such outlays are minimal relative to annual income, no serious hardship occurs and no special incentive is needed.

I, therefore, recommend that itemized deductions, which now average about 20 percent of adjusted gross incomes, be limited to those in excess of five percent of the taxpayer's adjusted gross income. This five percent floor will make $2.3 billion of revenue available for reduction in individual tax rates. At the same time incentives to home ownership or charitable contributions will remain. In fact, this tax program as a whole, providing as it does substantial reductions in Federal tax liabilities for virtually all families and individuals, will make it easier for people to meet their personal and civic obligations. This broadening of the tax base which Permits a greater reduction in individual income tax rates has an accompanying advantage of real simplification. An additional 6.5 million taxpayers will no longer itemize their deductions but still benefit overall from the reduced rates and other relief measures.

SIMPLIFICATION & SIMPLIFICATION OF THE MEDICAL EXPENSE DEDUCTION.

The medical expense deduction allowed to taxpayers who are under 65 years of age is limited to medical expenses in excess of three percent of their income. A separate floor of one percent of income is applicable to expenditures for drugs. In the interests of simplification, these two floors should be combined.

Under this recommendation, only those medical and drug expenses which together exceed four percent of income would be deductible. The qualifying expenses would, of course, along with other itemized deductions, be subject to the general five-percent floor. To lighten the burdens of our older citizens, all taxpayers who have reached the age of 65 should be relieved from the present one percent floor on drug expenses. They are already exempt from the three-percent floor on medical expenses. Under present law there is also a maximum limit on medical deductions of $5,000 for a single person and up to $20,000 for a married couple.

This maximum limit represents an anomaly in the law in that it prohibits the deduction of the truly catastrophic expenses for medical care and drugs that are sometimes incurred. I recommend, therefore, that the maximum limit be removed. Other amendments in the definition of certain medical and drug expenses, designed to prevent abuses, will be required in connection with these changes. The net revenue change as a result of these recommendations for simplification would involve an increase of $30 million - an insignificant part of the $6 billion of medical expense deductions which are taken today. Minor casualty losses.

Casualty losses on property are today fully deductible, without any floor comparable to that applicable to medical expenses to separate the extraordinary casualty from the average run of minor accidents. There is no reason why truly minor casualties-the inevitable dented fender, for example - should receive special treatment under the tax law. I, therefore, recommend that casualty losses enter into the calculation of itemized deductions only to the extent that they exceed four percent of the taxpayer's income.

The qualifying expenses would, of course, along with other itemized deductions, be subject to the general 570 floor. This recommendation will increase annual tax receipts by 190 million. Unlimited charitable deduction. Present law permits a handful of high income taxpayers to take an unlimited deduction for charitable contributions, instead of the an to 30 percent of income normally allowable.

These taxpayers for a number of years have made charitable contributions in an amount which, when added to their income tax liability, exceeds 90 percent of their taxable income - thus making the contribution fully deductible. Usually these contributions are made in substantially appreciated stock or other property. In this way the appreciation in value, without ever being subject to tax, constitutes a major part of the unlimited deduction. While naturally these generous contributions are beneficial, these taxpayers-given their otherwise high taxable income (up to several million dollars annually in some cases) - should not be escaping all Federal income tax as is the case today.

They should be limited to the same 30 percent deduction for charitable contributions as everyone else. Repeal of the unlimited charitable deduction would mean an annual revenue increase of $10 million. Repeal of the sick pay exclusion. Employees who are absent from work because of illness or injury may exclude from income subject to tax up to $100 a week received under employer-financed wage or salary continuation plans. This 'sick pay' exclusion is clearly unjustifiable. The taxpayer escapes tax on the salary he continues to receive, although his substantial medical expenses are deductible; and the employee who stays on the job, even though ill or injured, is in effect penalized for working. The sick pay exclusion which is of greatest benefit to those with large salary incomes and of far less value to most wage earners - should be repealed.

This action would provide $110 million per year in additional revenue. Exclusion of premiums on group term insurance. Neither the current value of group term life insurance protection nor the benefits received thereunder are now subject to tax if purchased for an employee by his employer.

This is, in effect, a valuable form of compensation, meeting the widespread desire to provide protection for one's family, which other taxpayers must pay for with after-tax dollars. I recommend that the current annual value to the employee of employer-financed group term life insurance protection be included in income, with an exception for the first $5,000 of coverage to correspond to the present exclusion for insured death benefits. Revenues would be increased by $60 million per year.

REPEAL OF THE DIVIDEND CREDIT AND EXCLUSION.

There is now allowed as an exclusion from income the first $50 of dividends received from domestic corporations, and in addition, a credit against tax equal to four percent of such dividend income in excess of $50. I repeat the recommendation made in my 1961 Tax Message that these provisions be repealed.

Proponents of the dividend credit and exclusion argued, in 1954, when these provisions were enacted, that they would encourage equity investment and provide a partial relief to the so-called double taxation of dividend income. Although these provisions involve an annual revenue loss at current levels of $460 million, they have failed to accomplish their objectives. The proportion of corporate funds secured from new equity financing has not increased; and the 'relief' gives the largest benefits to those with the highest incomes.

A far more equitable and effective means of accomplishing the objectives of the dividend credit and exclusion is to be found in my recommendation for reduction in the corporate income tax rate. The five-point reduction in that rate will reduce the tax differential against distributed corporate earnings by approximately 10 percent for all taxpayers.

The dividend credit, on the other hand, provides much less relief for taxpayers with taxable incomes of less than $180,000 (190,000 for single individuals) and greater relief only for the very highest income recipients. Moreover, since the benefits of the dividend credit and exclusion go largely to those in the middle and upper brackets, their repeal is necessary to justify the rate schedules I am recommending.

Should no action be taken on this recommendation, a higher

rate schedule designed to yield an additional $460 million from the middle and upper brackets would be appropriate. This would involve a rate structure scaled to a top rate of 70 percent rather than 65 percent, with appropriate changes in other brackets. Natural resources. We must continue to foster the efficient development of our mineral industries which have contributed so heavily to the economic progress of this nation.

At the same time, however, in the interest of both equity and the efficient allocation of capital, no one industry should be permitted to obtain an undue tax advantage over all others. Unintended defects have arisen in the application of the special tax privileges that Congress has granted to mineral industries, and correction of these defects is required if the existing tax provisions are to operate in a consistent and equitable fashion. The changes recommended below will alleviate this situation and yield an additional $300 million per year in revenue. The following areas in particular suggest the need for revision:

(a) CARRYOVER OF EXCESS DEDUCTIONS.

Under present tax law, mineral industries are permitted to deduct from taxable income a depletion allowance based on a percentage of gross mineral income but subject to a limit of 50 percent of net income from each producing property. The intent of this net income limit is not always realized, however, because substantial amounts of development costs and other expenses incurred while the property is being developed are not brought into the net income limit for the purpose of computing the depletion allowance, but are instead charged off against income from other sources.

The result is that in many cases percentage depletion far exceeds 50 percent of net income earned over the life of the property, when net income is properly defined to include development costs. One method of removing this defect in present law would be to provide that amounts in excess of gross income from the mineral property, which are deducted against other income of the taxpayer, should be used to reduce the net income from the property (for purposes of computing percentage depletion) in later producing years.

These carryover amounts could either be applied fully as the taxpayer obtains income from the property or be spread over several years. The deduction of drilling and development expenditures when made would not be affected; but, regardless of when they were made, they would be taken into account in computing the 50 percent of net income limitation on percentage depletion. This proposal would apply only to expenditures made in taxable years beginning after December 31, 1963.

(b) GROUPING OF PROPERTIES.

This same 50% limitation imposed by the Congress has also been minimized by the effect of legislation enacted in 1954, which permitted large oil and gas producers to pick and choose properties to be combined into an 'operating unit' for the purpose of computing depletion and reducing taxes. Percentage depletion historically has been corrupted separately for each mineral property. This grouping procedure has little or no business significance; and it benefits almost entirely companies with a large number of widely scattered mineral properties.

The original strength and purpose of the 50 percent limitation should be restored by returning to the rule that different oil and gas leases or acquisitions may not be combined for tax purposes, and that separate interests may be combined only if they are all on a single lease or acquisition. Such a change would bring tax rules regarding the grouping of properties into accord with business procedures.

(c) CAPITAL GAINS on sale of mineral interests. The Congress, in Section 13 of the Revenue Act of 1962, recognized that the owners of depreciable business assets were obtaining an unfair advantage by taking depreciation deductions against ordinary income greater than the actual loss in value, and then, upon the sale of an asset, paying only a capital gains tax on the recovery of these deductions.

The Congress, therefore, decided that any gains realized on the sale of such property should be taxed as ordinary income to the extent that the cost of the property has been deducted in the past - still permitting the excess of the sales price over the original cost to be treated as a capital gain. This same rule, which under my capital gains proposals discussed below would be extended to real estate and a variety of other situations, should also apply to mineral property subject to depletion, and would increase revenues by $50 million.

(d) FOREIGN OPERATIONS. Inasmuch as American firms engaged in oil, gas and mineral operations abroad are permitted the same depletion allowances and expensing of development costs as domestic producers, their United States tax on income from those operations is frequently smaller than the foreign tax they are entitled to credit.

The law should be amended to prevent an unused or excess foreign tax credit from being used to offset United States taxes on other forms or sources of foreign income. In addition, the deduction of foreign development costs should apply only to the income from those operations, and should not be permitted to reduce the United States tax on their domestic income. Action by the Congress in these four areas will adopt the most clearly justified steps needed to place the present system of depletion allowances in a more appropriate framework.

In addition, both the Administration and the appropriate committees of the Congress should study more closely the impact of the present percentage depletion rates and their applicability regardless of size or income on the development of our natural resources and the number of investors and producers attracted to the extractive industries. While these are complex as well as controversial problems, we cannot shrink from a frank appraisal of governmental policies and tax subsidies in this area.

Personal holding companies. The present restrictions upon the use of personal holding companies have been inadequate to prevent many high-bracket taxpayers from sheltering large amounts of passive investment income in corporations they own and control. By generating a relatively small amount of operating income, or through the use of rentals and royalties as a shield for dividend income, they have been able to avoid personal income taxes upon portfolio investments. I recommend that these provisions be tightened to end these escape routes which permit such passive investment income to be accumulated in closely held corporations at low rates of tax. Such action will increase annual tax revenue by $10 million.

(C) REVISION OF CAPITAL GAINS TAXATION.

The present tax treatment of capital gains and losses is both inequitable and a barrier to economic growth. With the exception of changes that have added various ordinary income items to the definition of statutory capital gains, there have been no significant changes in this area of the income tax since 1942. The tax on capital gains directly affects investment decisions, the mobility and flow of risk capital from static to more dynamic situations, the ease or difficulty experienced by new ventures in obtaining capital, and thereby the strength and potential for growth of the economy.

The provisions for taxation of capital gains are in need of essential changes designed to facilitate the attainment of our economic objectives. I therefore, recommend the following changes, the nature of which requires their consideration as a unified package, coupling liberalization of treatment with more sensible and equitable limitations: Percentage inclusion. Reduce the percentage of long term capital gains included in individual income subject to tax from the present 50 percent of the gain to 30 percent.

Combined with the proposed individual income tax rate schedule ranging from 14 to 65 percent, this will produce capital gains tax rates that will start at 4.2 percent (instead of the present 10 percent) and progress to a maximum of 19.5 percent (instead of the present 25 percent). With the enactment of this recommendation, the same ratio will exist for all income groups between the tax rate payable on ordinary income and the tax rate payable on capital gains - which is not the case at the present time. The present 25 percent alternative tax on the capital gains of corporations should be reduced to 22 percent as a part of the reduction of the corporate normal tax rate to 22 percent.

This will greatly simplify tax accounting for the more than half a million small corporations subject only to the normal tax. Holding period. Extend the minimum holding period for qualifying for long-term capital gains treatment from the present six months to one year. Preferential capital gains treatment with respect to gains on assets held less than one year cannot be justified either in terms of long-run economic objectives or equity. Moreover, the present six-months test makes it relatively easy to convert various types of what is actually ordinary income into capital gains.

This proposal will provide far greater assurance that capital gains treatment is confined to bona fide investors rather than to short-term speculators. The new lower rates of ordinary income tax, which will apply to gains realized on holdings of less than six months as well as six months to one year, will mitigate the reduced rate of turnover of securities and other assets that might otherwise result.

CARRYOVER OF CAPITAL LOSSES.

Permit an indefinite carryover of capital losses incurred by an individual in any one year. Under present law capital losses may be carried over for only five years. They may be charged against ordinary income in an amount of up to $1,000 in each of the five years and against capital gains. The five-year limitation frequently works serious hardships on investors, particularly small investors, who incur substantial capital losses and do not within five years have the opportunity to realize gains sufficiently large to absorb them. More adequate capital loss offsets will improve the investment odds, encourage risk-taking on the part of investors, and stimulate economic growth.

Tax treatment of gains accrued on capital assets at the time of gift or death. Impose a tax at capital gains rates on all net gains accrued on capital assets at the time of transfer at death or by gift. Adoption of this proposal is an essential element of my program for the taxation of capital gains; certainly in its absence there would be no justification for any reduction of present capital gain rate schedules. A number of exceptions would limit the applicability of this proposal to fewer than three percent of those who die each year.

These exceptions would provide special rules for the transfer of household and personal effects, assets transferred to a surviving wife or husband, and a certain minimum amount of property in every case. Appreciation on property subject to the charitable contribution deduction would continue to be exempt both on gift and at death. For those who would have a substantial amount of appreciation taxed upon transfer at death, a special averaging provision would prevent the application of higher rates than would have applied upon disposition over a period of years.

In addition, it should be clearly understood that the tax upon transfer at death would reduce the size of the taxable estate, and thereby reduce the estate tax. The present provisions for extended payment of estate taxes would apply to the new taxes upon appreciated property transferred at death and would be liberalized. My proposal, if enacted, would apply to gifts made after this date, but would be phased to apply fully to transfers at death only after three years.

The Secretary of the Treasury will present a technical elaboration of this proposal and its relationship to the existing rules for the taxation of various kinds of assets transferred at death. Definitional changes. The wartime increase in the income tax rate structure led to repeated efforts to obtain extension of capital gains treatment to a variety of sources of ordinary income. In some cases this treatment was related to the very high rates of tax on ordinary income. In such cases capital gains treatment is no longer appropriate.

In some other cases the justification given for the special treatment was the desire to give a special subsidy to the industry concerned. In other situations, as mentioned earlier with respect to mineral properties, many taxpayers have been able to profit through claiming deductions against ordinary income for expenses, interest, depreciation or depletion, which are later recovered on disposition of property at much lower capital gain rates. The existing sprawling scope of this preferential treatment has led to serious economic distortions and has encouraged tax avoidance maneuvers sometimes characterized as the 'capital gains route.'

This trend should now be reversed, particularly because of the benefits of the lower capital gains rates as well as lower personal tax rates which I am recommending. Wherever the case for a special subsidy is not compelling, the definitions should be changed to limit capital gains to those transactions which clearly merit such treatment. The details regarding specific proposals in this area will be presented by the Secretary of the Treasury. They will include, but not be limited to, the following:

a. Real estate tax shelters, which are giving rise to increasingly uneconomic investment practices and are threatening legitimate real estate developments; and

b. The tax treatment of restricted stock options.

The difference between the price paid for optioned stock at the time of exercise of such an option and the option price represents compensation for services quite as much as do wages and salaries. Under present law, however, such gains are taxed under capital gains rules at very favorable rates and the tax liability may be postponed for many years.

Under present war-inspired high tax rates, compensation arrangements of this kind clearly have their attractions. But under the new, more reasonable rates I am recommending, the favored tax treatment of stock options can no longer be said to be either desirable or necessary; and larger salary payments will be more effective than at present as a means of attracting and holding corporate executives.

I, therefore, recommend that, with respect to stock options granted after this date, the spread between the option price and the value of the stock at the date the option is exercised be taxed at ordinary income tax rates at the time the option is exercised. The averaging provision referred to above which the Secretary of the Treasury will present will prevent a tax penalty due to bunching of income in one year. In addition, payment of tax attributable to exercise of the stock option would be permitted in installments over several years.

This change will remove a gross inequality in the application of the income tax, but it is not expected to yield appreciable amounts of revenue; for the gains to be taxed as compensation to the employee will, as in the case of compensation in other forms, be deductible from the income of the employer. The overall effect of all these changes in the capital gain provisions affecting individuals and corporations will stimulate a freer flow of investment funds and facilitate economic growth as well as provide more evenhanded treatment of taxpayers across the board.

They have a direct positive revenue impact of about $100 million per year. The reduction in the tax rate on capital gains will be somewhat more than offset by the increased revenue from the change in holding period, the taxation of capital gains at death and the changes in definitions - including those affecting real estate shelters and sales of mineral properties. However, the 'lock-in' effect of the present law, due to the ability to avoid all capital gains taxes on assets held until death, will be eliminated.

This will result in a sharp increase in transfers of capital assets as individuals feel free to shift to the most desirable investment. The increased volume of transactions under these new rules should, in an average year, yield approximately $700 million in additional revenue. Indeed, this figure will be substantially higher during the first few years after enactment as those who are presently 'locked-in' respond to the new situation.

VII. SUMMARY/ CONCLUSION.

The foregoing program of rate reduction and reform provides for a fair and comprehensive net reduction in tax liabilities at all levels of income. As shown in the attached Table 3, the overall savings are proportionately highest at the lower end of the income scale, where for taxpayers with adjusted gross incomes of less than $3,000 the reduction is nearly 40%. As we move up the income scale, the percentage reduction in tax liabilities declines to slightly less than 10 percent for taxpayers with incomes in excess of $50,000.

For all groups of taxpayers combined, the reduction is approximately 18 percent, but five out of six taxpayers - most of whom have incomes below $10,000 - will enjoy a reduction of more than 20 percent. In addition, the proposed reforms will go a long way toward simplifying the problem of filling out tax returns for the more than 60 million fliers each year. Under these proposals more than 6 million people will no longer find necessary the record-keeping and detailed accounting required by itemized deductions.

Hundreds of thousands of older people and individuals and families with very low incomes will no longer be required to file any tax returns at all. Special tax problems of small business, the aged, working mothers and low-income groups are effectively met. Special preferences for capital gains, natural resources, excessive deductions and other areas outside the tax base are curbed.

Both the mobility and the formation of capital are encouraged. The lower corporate tax rates will encourage and stimulate business enterprise. The reduction of the top 91% rate will assist investment and risk-taking. Above all, by expanding both consumer demand and investment, this program will raise production and income, provide jobs for the unemployed, and take up the slack in our economy.

Members of the Congress:

There is general agreement among those in business and labor most concerned that this Nation requires major tax revision, involving both net tax reduction and base-broadening reform. There is also general agreement that this should be enacted as promptly as is consistent with orderly legislative process. Differences which may arise will be largely those of degree and emphasis. I hope that, having examined these differences, the Congress will enact this year a modification of our tax laws along the general lines I have proposed. To repeat what I said in my Message on the State of the Union. - Now is the time to act. We cannot afford to be timid or slow. For this is the most urgent task confronting the Congress in 1963.

JOHN F. KENNEDY, FEBRUARY 21, 1963, MESSAGE ON NEEDS OF NATION'S SENIOR CITIZENS:

The tax program I recently submitted to the Congress will, by calendar year 1965, reduce Federal income tax liabilities for an estimated 3.4 million persons aged 65 and over by $790 million. An estimated $470 million of this reduction will arise from the general rate reductions and certain other provisions affecting the aged. The other $320 million reduction results from the replacement of the present complicated retirement income credit and extra exemption with a flat $300 tax credit.[80]

JOHN F. KENNEDY, JULY 17, 1963, THE PRESIDENT'S NEWS CONFERENCE:

Tax collections are also better than we estimated in January. But we still have too many idle plants and jobless workers. The recent improvement in business conditions has contributed to these higher revenues. This demonstrates again the point which I emphasized in my tax message to the Congress. Rising tax receipts and eventual elimination of budget deficits depend primarily on a healthy and rapidly growing economy.

The most urgent economic business before the Nation is a prompt and substantial reduction and revision of Federal income taxes in order to speed up our economic growth and wipe out our present excessive unemployment. A prosperous and growing economy is a major objective in its own right. It is also the primary means by which to achieve a balance in our Federal budget and in our balance of payments.[81]

JOHN F. KENNEDY, SEPTEMBER 18, 1963, RADIO & TV ADDRESS ON THE TAX REDUCTION BILL:

The Federal income tax is one of those subjects about which we talk, about which we complain, but about which not very much is done. Perhaps we have heard too long about the certainty of 'death and taxes.' Perhaps other national and international issues now seem more pressing. Yet, the fact is that the high wartime and postwar tax rates we are now paying are no longer necessary. They are, in fact, harmful.

These high rates do not leave enough money in private hands to keep this country's economy growing and healthy. They have helped to cause recessions in previous years, including 1958 and 1960, and unless they are reduced, they can cause recessions again. The bill on which the House will vote next week is a sound bill and we need it for many reasons.

FIRST, a tax cut means more jobs for American workers; more after tax money means more buying power for consumers and investors; and this means more production and the jobs our Nation needs. Merely to reduce unemployment to a more acceptable level in the next 2 1/2 years, we must create more than 10,000 new jobs every day. We cannot effectively attack the problem of teenage crime and delinquency as long as so many of our young people are out of work. We cannot effectively solve the problem of racial injustice as long as unemployment is high. We cannot tackle the problem of automation when we are losing 1 million jobs every year to machines.

SECOND, a tax cut means new protection against another tragic recession. I do not say that a recession is inevitable without a tax .cut, or impossible with one, but, excluding war years, we have had a recession on the average every 42 months since World War II, or every 44 months since World War I, and by next January it will be 44 months since the last recession began. Recessions mean high unemployment and high budget deficits. Of all kinds of waste, they are the worst. We need a tax cut to keep this present drive from running out of gas...

THIRD, a tax cut means new markets for American business. American citizens will spend, as history shows us, an overwhelming percentage of the extra, after tax dollars left in their pockets, and this spending will broaden markets for businessmen, put idle machines to work, and require new machines and new factories to be built. The multiplied effect of these new private consumption and investment expenditures released by the tax cut will create a new market right here at home nearly equal to the gross national product of Canada and Australia combined.

FOURTH, a tax cut means higher family income and higher business profits and a balanced Federal budget. Every taxpayer and his family will have more money left over after taxes for a new car, a new home, new conveniences, education, and investment. Every businessman can keep a higher percentage of his profits in his cash register or put it to work expanding or improving his business, and as the national income grows, the Federal Government will ultimately end up with more revenues. Prosperity is the real way to balance our budget.

Our tax rates are so high today that the growth of profits and pay checks in this country have been stunted. Our tax revenues have been depressed and our books for out of the last 10 years have been in the red. By lowering tax rates, by increasing jobs and income, we can expand tax revenues and bring finally our budget into balance, and to assist further in this effort we have pledged an even tighter rein on Federal expenditures, limiting our outlays to those activities which are fully essential to the Nation. Spending will be controlled and our deficit will be reduced.

FIFTH, and finally, a tax cut means new strength around the world for the American dollar and for freedom. A tax cut can help us balance our international accounts and end the outflow of gold by helping make the American economy more efficient and more productive and more competitive, by enabling our goods to compete with those who are developing foreign factories, and by making investment in America more attractive than investment abroad.

And a tax cut will help us convince other countries of the advantages of freedom by helping to end the longterm poverty, of chronic unemployment and depressed areas which mark our country.

FOR ALL THESE REASONS, this bill deserves your support. I do not say it will solve all of our economic problems; no single measure can do that. We need to advance on many other fronts, on education, in job retraining, in area redevelopment, in youth employment, and the rest, but this bill is the keystone of the arch. Of course, it is always possible to find fault with any bill, to suggest delays or to attach reservations.

It is always possible for someone to say, 'I am for the tax cut if other conditions are met, or when certain changes have been made, or some other versions at some future time,' but if we are to make the most of what this bill has to offer in creating jobs, in fighting recession, and balancing our international payments, it must not be diluted by amendments or conditions. It must not be sent back to the House Ways and Means Committee. it must not be put off until next year.

This Nation needs a tax cut now, not a tax cut if and when, but a tax cut now, and for the future. This Nation needs a tax cut now that will benefit every family, every business, in every part of the Nation. Some of you may not be fully aware of the problems of those who face unemployment. Most families are doing better than ever. Another recession or the pains of economic insecurity or deprivation may seem very far away tonight, but they are not so far away if you look around your neighborhood or this country of ours.

If you live in a growing community or a prosperous neighborhood, see for yourself the conditions of those who cannot find work, those who live in depression. If your son is in high school or college, take a look at the plight of those who have dropped out and the millions of young people pouring into our labor markets. Seven million more young people will come into the labor market in the sixties than did in the fifties, and we have to find work for them.

Your children will be aware of this when they go to find a job. Life looks rosy to those with highly trained skills that are in widespread demand, but we must not forget about the less trained and the less skilled who may not be in demand. If we cannot create more jobs, and let me emphasize again, to get unemployment down to an acceptable level in the next 2 1/2 years we need 10 million new jobs - where are we going to find them? I think we can only find them if the economy of this country grows as it must, and that is why I propose this bill tonight.

If we permit unemployment to grow, if we move into another recession, then no worker can be sure of his job and no businessman can be sure of his future, and nobody can point to the United States as a vital, dynamic economy. So I ask you to consider the hopes and fears of those out of work in your own community and in your country, whether they are very young or very old, Negro or white, in need of training or retraining.

A tax cut will help them to find jobs. It will help everyone increase his income and it will help prevent the spread of unemployment. There are, in fact, as many people out of work today, men and women in this country of ours, in a prosperous year, as there have been in some recession years.

We are the only country, nearly, in the West which has such a large percentage of unemployed. We get properly excited about a labor dispute which idles thousands of workers, but our loss from excessive unemployment in recent years has been 20 times as great as our loss from strikes, and I say again in the next 2 1/2 years we need 10,000 new jobs every day for a total of 10 million jobs.

That is what this tax cut can help to give us. That is why this problem affects every citizen and that is why this bill provides, from top to bottom, across-the-board tax reduction on both personal and corporate income. Under this bill, every wage earner in the country will take home more money every week beginning January 1st. Every businessman will pay a lower tax rate.

Low income families and small businessmen will get a special tax relief, and the unemployed worker who gets a new job will find his income going up many times. Here is how it will work: A factory earner with three dependents earning $90 a week will have his taxes reduced by a third.

The typical American family, a father, mother, and two children, earning about $6,000 a year, now pays an annual tax of $600. This bill will cut that tax by 25 percent. A salaried employee with a wife and two children who earns $8,000 a year will receive a tax cut of more than 20 percent that will enable him perhaps to pay the installments on a car or a dishwasher or some other necessary expense, thereby creating work for others.

These individual benefits, of course, are important, but the most important benefit goes to the Nation as a whole. As these typical families, and millions like them across our country, spend that extra money on dishwashers, or clothes, or a washing machine, or an encyclopedia, or a longer vacation trip, or a down payment on a new car or a new home, that is what makes jobs. The businesses which serve them need to hire more men and women.

The men and women who are hired have more money to spend. The companies who sell these items have more incentive to invest, to improve, and to expand their operation. More young people out of school can find work and the danger of recession then becomes less. Recessions, as I have said, in this country have been too harmful and too frequent, and have become more so. Between the first and second postwar recession, we had 45 months of upturn. Between the second and third, 35 months.

Between the third and fourth, 25 months. We have now had 31 months of steady upturn. I would like to see us skip a recession. I would like to see us release $11 billion of after-tax purchasing power into the private economy before another downturn can begin. That is why this bill is insurance for prosperity and insurance against recession. Recessions am not inevitable.

They have not occurred in Europe for 10 years, and I believe that some day in this country we can wipe them out. We already have the ability to reduce their frequency, their importance, and their duration, and this tax cut is the single most important weapon that we can now add. The support in this country for a tax cut crosses political lines. It includes small businessmen, workers and farmers, economists, and educators. Very few are openly opposed, of course, to cutting taxes, but there are those who for one reason or another hope to delay this bill, or to attach ruinous amendments, or to water down its effects.

They want to deny our country the full benefits of tax reduction because they say there is waste in Government. There may be, and we are working to get rid of it, but let us not forget the waste in 4 million unemployed men and women, with a prospect of still more unemployment if this bill does not pass. There are those who talk about inflation when, in fact, prices have been steady, wholesale prices have been wholly steady for the last 5 years - a record unmatched in our history and unmatched in any other country - and when persistent slack in our economy threatens us far more with recession than with inflation.

Those who are opposed talk about the Federal debt, when the actual burden of that debt on our economy is being steadily reduced. Since World War II, the national debt has gone up 11 percent while our national output has gone up nearly 300 percent in contrast to State and local government, which has risen nearly 400 percent-their debt - in the same period as opposed to the Federal Government's 11 percent.

Those who are opposed to this bill talk about skyrocketing Federal employment when, in fact, we have steadily reduced the number of Federal employees serving every 1000 people in this country. In fact, there are fewer Federal civilian employees today than there were 10 years ago. We have reduced waste and improved efficiency at the Pentagon and in the Post Office, in the farm programs, and in other agencies throughout the Government. Section 1 of this bill, as Chairman Mills of the House Ways and Means Committee pointed out, makes clear that voting for this bill is a choice of tax reduction, instead of deliberate deficits, as the principal means of boosting the economy and finding jobs for our people.

No wasteful, inefficient or unnecessary Government activity will be tolerated. We are pledged to a course of true fiscal responsibility, leading to a balanced budget in a balanced, full-employment economy. My fellow citizens, this is a matter which affects our country and its future. We are talking about more jobs; we are talking about the future of our country, about its strength and growth and stability as the leader of the free world.

We are talking about helping people, people who have been looking for work for a long time in Eastern Kentucky, in West Virginia and Pennsylvania, the steel towns of Ohio, Gary, Indiana, Southern Illinois, other parts of our country, some of our mill towns; we are talking about a tax cut in the pockets of our people that will help create jobs and income for everyone.

We are talking, as I said at the start, about one of the most important pieces of legislation to come before the Congress this year-the most important domestic economic measure to come before the Congress in 15 years. That bill could be weakened or deferred. It could be put off for another year. It could be cut down. It needs your support. This is not a question of party. It is a question of the growth of our country, of the jobs and security of our people.

It is a question of whether our taxpayers and businessmen and workers will get the help they deserve. As the Congress prepares next week to vote on this measure, I strongly urge you to support this bill for your family's sake and for your country's sake.[82]

JOHN F. KENNEDY, NOVEMBER 18, 1963, BEFORE FLORIDA CHAMBER OF COMMERCE:

A little more than a year ago, when our bill to grant a tax credit for business investment was before the Congress, Secretary of the Treasury Dillon was on a plane to this State, and he found himself talking to one of the leading Florida businessmen about the investment tax credit. He spent some time, he later told me, explaining how the bill would help this man's corporate outlook and income, and the businessman was most impressed.

Finally, as the plane landed at Miami, he turned to Secretary Dillon and said, 'I am very grateful to you for explaining the bill. Now tell me just once more: why is it I am against it?' That story is unfortunately not an exaggeration. Many businessmen, who are prospering as never before during this administration, are convinced nevertheless that we must be anti-business. With the new figures on corporate profits after taxes having reached an all-time high, running some 43 percent higher than they were just 3 years ago, they still suspect us of being opposed to private profit. With the most stable price level of any comparable economic recovery in our history, they still fear that we are promoting inflation.

We have liberalized depreciation guidelines to grant more individual flexibility, reduced our farm surpluses, reduced transportation taxes, established a private corporation to manage our satellite communication system, increased the role of American business in the development of less developed countries, and proposed to the Congress a sharp reduction in corporate as well as personal income taxes, and a major deregulation of transportation, and yet many businessmen are convinced that a Democratic administration is out to soak the rich, increase controls for the sake of controls, and extend at all costs the scope of the Federal bureaucracy. The hard facts contradict these doubts.

This administration is interested in the healthy expansion of the entire economy. We are interested in the steady progress of our entire society. And it is in this kind of program, in my opinion, in which American business has the largest stake. Why is it that profits are at an all-time high in the Nation today? It is because the Nation as a whole is prospering. It is because our gross national product is rising from $500 billion to $600 billion, a record rise of $100 billion in 3 years, 36 months. It is because industrial production in the last 3 years has increased 22 percent, and personal income by 15 percent. It is because, as the Wall Street Journal pointed out last week, the United States now leads most of Western Europe in the rate of business expansion.

For the first time in many years, in the last 18 months our growth rate exceeds that of France or Germany. It is because, as Fortune magazine recently pointed out, corporate profits in America are now rising much faster than corporate profits overseas. It is because these profits have not been eaten up by an inflationary spiral. And finally, it is because we have reversed the dismal trend towards even more frequent recessions which are the greatest enemy of profits. By next April, with the indispensable help of the pending tax cut bill, the United States will be sailing with the winds of the longest and strongest peacetime economic expansion in our Nation's entire history. I do not say that all this is due to the administration alone, but neither is it all accidental.

The fiscal and monetary policies which we have followed are the key elements in whether the economy moves toward a path of expansion or restriction. In the last 3 years, American business and industry have directly benefited from a host of our legislative and administrative actions which increased corporate tax flow, increased markets at home and abroad, increased consumer purchasing power, and increased plant modernization and productivity.

And still other steps have been taken to curb the wage-price spiral - the first 6 months of 1963 there was less time lost in strikes than any time since the Second World War - to hold down the cost of credit, and to bring more harmony into industrial relations. I do not say that these actions were taken for the benefit of business alone.

They were taken to benefit the country. Some of them were labeled pro-business, some of them were labeled anti-business, some of them were labeled both by opposing groups. But that kind of label is meaningless. This administration is 'pro' the public interest. Nor do I say that all of these policies could please all American businessmen all of the time. So long as the interest and views of businessmen frequently clash with each other, no President could possibly please them all.

Most businessmen, though perhaps not most business spokesmen, are associated with small business. They ask the Government for assistance to protect them against monopoly, to assure them of reasonable credit, to enable them to participate in defense contracts. And both large and small business work with the various arms of the administration every day on trade, transportation, procurement, balance of payments, and international business affairs.

They do not show the hostility which is so often described or find that our policies and personnel are so incompatible with their own. Businessmen are welcome at the White House, and I welcome the chance to address business meetings such as this, not because I expect that it will necessarily affect the results of the elections, but I do think it can affect what this country does and how it moves ahead, and whether we are going to be able to find jobs for all the people that need them, and whether we are going to build the kind of a country in which all of us can take pride and credit.

And that is the kind of cooperative effort which I invite from businessmen and from other interested citizens. If we can keep open the channels of communication, this country can make progress ahead. To further that understanding, I would like to answer four questions that I am most frequently asked by businessmen or written about or written to.[83]

JOHN F. KENNEDY, NOVEMBER 22, 1963, REMARKS PREPARED FOR DELIVERY AT THE TRADE MART IN DALLAS, TX:

It is clear, therefore, that we are strengthening our security as well as our economy by our recent record increases in national income and output by surging ahead of most of Western Europe in the rate of business expansion and the margin of corporate profits, by maintaining a more stable level of prices than almost any of our overseas competitors, and by cutting personal and corporate income taxes by some $11 billion, as I have proposed, to assure this Nation of the longest and strongest expansion in our peacetime economic history.

This Nation's total output, which 3 years ago was at the $500 billion mark will soon pass $600 billion, for a record rise of over $100 billion in 3 years. For the first time in history we have 70 million men and women at work. For the first time in history average factory earnings have exceeded $100 a week. For the first time in history corporation profits after taxes which have risen 43 percent in less than 3 years have an annual level of $27.4 billion.[84]

ENDNOTES

1. James Earl 'Jimmy' Carter, Jr. July 15, 1976, Democratic acceptance speech, delivered in Madison Square Garden, New York City. Vital Speeches, August 15, 1976. The Annals of America, 20 vols. (Chicago, IL: Encyclopedia Britannica, 1968, 1977), Vol. 20, pp. 348-351.

2. Congressman J.C. Watts, Jr (R-OK). Feb. 5, 1997, Library of Congress, Washington, D.C., televised Republican response to President Clinton's State of the Union Address.

3. John Steele Gordon, 'American Taxation - How a Nation born out of a Tax Revolt has - and especially hasn't - solved the problems of taxing its citizens' (American Heritage, May/June 1996), pp. 63-86.

4. Isaac Backus. Sept. 1775, Address to Massachusetts Assembly, in behalf of the Warren Association, on the subject of taxing religious dissenters. A Church History of New-England (Providence, 1784), p. 305. The Annals of America, 20 vols. (Chicago, IL: Encyclopedia Britannica, 1968), Vol. 2, p. 366.

5. Declaration of Independence. July 4, 1776. American Historical Documents - Harvard Classics, 50 volumes (New York: P.F. Collier & Son Company, 1910), Vol. 43, p. 160.

6. Articles of Confederation. July 9, 1778; March 1, 1781, Article VIII, Section 2. Michael Farris, Constitutional Law - Original Documents & Decisions of the U.S. Supreme Court (Paeonian Springs, VA: Home School Legal Defense Association, 1991), Chap. 3, p. 25.

7. Andrew Jackson. Dec. 5, 1836, 8th Annual Message. James D. Richardson (U.S. Representative from Tennessee), ed., A Compilation of the Messages & Papers of the Presidents 1789-1897, 10 vols. (Wash., D.C.: U.S. Gov. Printing Office, published by Authority of Congress, 1897, 1899; Wash., D.C.: Bureau of National Literature & Art, 1789-1902, 11 vols., 1907, 1910), Vol. II, pp. 236, 240-241, 243-244, 260.

8. United States Constitution. Sept. 17, 1787, Article I, Section 8.1. American Historical Documents - Harvard Classics, 50 vol. (New York: P.F. Collier & Son Co. 1910), Vol. 43, p. 196.

9. United States Constitution. Sept. 17, 1787, Article I, Section 8.1. American Historical Documents - Harvard Classics, 50 vol. (New York: P.F. Collier & Son Co., 1910), Vol. 43, p. 196.

10. Thomas Jefferson. Dec. 15, 1802, 2nd Annual Message. James D. Richardson (U.S. Representative from Tennessee), ed., A Compilation of the Messages & Papers of the Presidents 1789-1897, 10 vols. (Wash., D.C.: U.S. Gov. Printing Office, pub. by Authority of Congress, 1897, 1899; Wash., D.C.: Bureau of Nat. Lit. & Art, 1789-1902, 11 vols., 1907, 1910), Vol. I, pp. 342-345.

11. John Fitzgerald Kennedy. Nov. 20, 1962, President's News Conference. Public Papers of the Presidents-Containing Public Messages, Speeches & Statements of the President, (Wash., DC: U.S. Gov. Printing Office.)

12. John Fitzgerald Kennedy. Jan. 17, 1963, Annual Budget Message, Fiscal Year 1964). Public Papers of the Presidents-Containing Public Messages, Speeches & Statements of the President, (Wash., DC: U.S. Gov. Printing Office.)

13. John Fitzgerald Kennedy. Jan. 21, 1963, Annual Message: The Economic Report of the President. Public Papers of the Presidents-Containing Public Messages, Speeches & Statements of the President, (Wash., DC: U.S. Gov. Printing Office.)

14. John Fitzgerald Kennedy. Jan. 21, 1963, Annual Message. The Economic Report of the President). Public Papers of the Presidents-Containing Public Messages, Speeches & Statements of the President, (Wash., DC: U.S. Gov. Printing Office.)

15. John Fitzgerald Kennedy. Jan. 24, 1963, Special Message on Tax Reduction & Reform, House Document 43, 88th Cong., 1st sess.). Public Papers of the Presidents-Containing Public Messages, Speeches & Statements of the President, (Wash., DC: U.S. Gov. Printing Office.)

16. John Fitzgerald Kennedy. Sept. 18, 1963, Radio & Television Address on the Test Ban Treaty & the Tax Reduction Bill). Public Papers of the Presidents-Containing Public Messages, Speeches & Statements of the President, (Wash., DC: U.S. Gov. Printing Office.)

17. John Fitzgerald Kennedy. Sept. 18, 1963, Radio & Television Address on the Test Ban Treaty & the Tax Reduction Bill). Public Papers of the Presidents-Containing Public Messages, Speeches & Statements of the President, (Wash., DC: U.S. Gov. Printing Office.)

18. Andrew Jackson. Dec. 5, 1836, 8th Annual Message. James D. Richardson (U.S. Representative from Tennessee), ed., A Compilation of the Messages & Papers of the Presidents 1789-1897, 10 vols. (Wash., D.C.: U.S. Gov. Printing Office, published by Authority of Congress, 1897, 1899; Wash., D.C.: Bureau of National Literature & Art, 1789-1902, 11 vols., 1907, 1910), Vol. II, pp. 236, 240-241, 243-244, 260.

19. John Marshall. 1819, case of McCulloch v. Maryland, 4 Wheaton 316, 431. John Bartlett, Bartlett's Familiar Quotations (Boston: Little, Brown & Company, 1855, 1980), p. 402.

20. Andrew Jackson. May 27, 1830, Veto Message. James D. Richardson (U.S. Representative from Tennessee), ed., A Compilation of the Messages & Papers of the Presidents 1789-1897, 10 vols. (Wash., D.C.: U.S. Gov. Printing Office, published by Authority of Congress, 1897, 1899; Wash., D.C.: Bureau of National Literature & Art, 1789-1902, 11 vols., 1907, 1910), Vol. II, p. 489.

21. Andrew Jackson. Dec. 5, 1836, 8th Annual Message. James D. Richardson (U.S. Representative from Tennessee), ed., A Compilation of the Messages &

Papers of the Presidents 1789-1897, 10 vols. (Wash., D.C.: U.S. Gov. Printing Office, published by Authority of Congress, 1897, 1899; Wash., D.C.: Bureau of National Literature & Art, 1789-1902, 11 vols., 1907, 1910), Vol. II, pp. 236, 240-241, 243-244, 260.

22. Andrew Jackson. March 4, 1837, Farewell Address. James D. Richardson (U.S. Representative from Tennessee), ed., A Compilation of the Messages & Papers of the Presidents 1789-1897, 10 vols. (Wash., D.C.: U.S. Gov. Printing Office, published by Authority of Congress, 1897, 1899; Wash., D.C.: Bureau of National Literature & Art, 1789-1902, 11 vols., 1907, 1910), Vol. II, pp. 292-308. The Annals of America, 20 vols. (Chicago, IL: Encyclopedia Britannica, 1968), Vol. VI, p. 310.

23. Franklin Pierce. Dec. 5, 1853, 1st Annual Message. James D. Richardson (U.S. Representative from Tennessee), ed., A Compilation of the Messages & Papers of the Presidents 1789-1897, 10 vols. (Wash., D.C.: U.S. Gov. Printing Office, published by Authority of Congress, 1897, 1899; Wash., D.C.: Bureau of Nat. Lit.& Art, 1789-1902, 11 vols., 1907, 1910), Vol. 5, pp. 207, 213.

24. Bureau of Internal Revenue. established 1862. John Steele Gordon, American Taxation - How a Nation born out of a Tax Revolt has - and especially hasn't - solved the problems of taxing its citizens? (American Heritage, May/June 1996), pp. 74. John Steele Gordon, American Taxation - How a Nation born out of a Tax Revolt has - and especially hasn't - solved the problems of taxing its citizens? (American Heritage, May/June 1996), pp. 72.

25. John Steele Gordon, American Taxation - How a Nation born out of a Tax Revolt has - and especially hasn't - solved the problems of taxing its citizens? (American Heritage, May/June 1996), pp. 72.

26. Karl Marx. Critique of the Gotha Programme 1875. USSR Constitution, 1917, Article 12, USSR Constitution, 1977, Article 14. 'From each according to his abilities, to each according to his work'. - from the Soviet Constitution of 1936. This phrase amended an article of the first Russian constitution which had been enacted after their revolution around 1918. The original article stated 'he who does not work, neither shall he eat'. In the Soviet (Stalin) Constitution of 1936, the 'from each' clause was added onto that article as a 'principle of socialism': Article 12 Work in the U.S.S.R. is a duty and a matter of honour for every able-bodied citizen, in accordance with the principle: 'He who does not work, neither shall he eat.' The principle applied in the U.S.S.R. is that of socialism: 'From each according to his ability, to each according to his work.' The 1977 Soviet Constitution contained it as follows: Article 14 (1) The source of the growth of social wealth and of the well-being of the people, and of each individual, is the labor, free from exploitation, of Soviet people. (2) The state exercises control over the measure of labor and of consumption in accordance with the principle of socialism: 'From each according to his ability, to each according to his work'. It fixes the rate of taxation on taxable income. (3) Socially useful work

and its results determine a person's status in society. By combining material and moral incentives and encouraging innovation and a creative attitude to work, the state helps transform labor into the prime vital need of every Soviet citizen. http://dhm.best.vwh.net/each.html http://www.visi.com/~contra_m/pc/ 1958/4-4socialist.html http://www.brainyquote.com/quotes/authors/k/ karl_marx.html http://www.geocities.com/commlin/quotations.html

27. Karl Marx: 'The theory of the Communists may be summed up in the single sentence: Abolition of private property.' http://www.brainyquote.com/quotes/authors/k/karl_marx.html

28. Senator John Sherman. John Steele Gordon, American Taxation - How a Nation born out of a Tax Revolt has - and especially hasn't - solved the problems of taxing its citizens? (American Heritage, May/June 1996), pp. 74 .

29. Felix Adler, founder of the Ethical Culture movement. John Steele Gordon, American Taxation - How a Nation born out of a Tax Revolt has - and especially hasn't - solved the problems of taxing its citizens? (American Heritage, May/June 1996), pp. 74.

30. United States Supreme Court. 1895, Chief Justice Melville W. Fuller, case of Pollock v. Farmers' Loan & Trust Co., 157, U.S. 429, 574 (1895), declaring income tax unconstitutional. Harold M. Groves, University of Wisconsin, Financing Government - Revised Edition (New York: Henry Holt & Co. Inc., 1939, 1945), p. 156. The court consisted of Chief Justice Melville W. Fuller, Ill.; Justice David Josiah Brewer, Kan.; Justice Horace Gray, Mass.; Justice John M. Harlan, Ky.; Justice Henry B. Brown, Mich.; Justice Stephen J. Field, Ca.; Justice George Shiras, Jr., Pa.; Justice Howell E. Jackson, Tenn.; and Justice Edward D. White, La.

31. United States Supreme Court. 1895, Justice Stephen J. Field, case of Pollock v. Farmers' Loan & Trust Co., 157, U.S. 429, 574 (1895), declaring income tax unconstitutional. Harold M. Groves, Univ. of Wisconsin, Financing Government - Revised Edition (New York: Henry Holt & Co., Inc., 1939, 1945), p. 156.

32. Theodore Roosevelt. John Steele Gordon, American Taxation - How a Nation born out of a Tax Revolt has - and especially hasn't - solved the problems of taxing its citizens? (American Heritage, May/June 1996), pp. 74. 'An income tax stands on an entirely different footing from an inheritance tax; because it involves no question of the perpetuation of fortunes swollen to an unhealthy size.' - Theodore Roosevelt, Dec. 3, 1906, 6th Annual Message. 'No advantage comes either to the country as a whole or to the individuals inheriting the money by permitting the transmission in their entirety of the enormous fortunes which would be affected by such a tax.' - Theodore Roosevelt, Dec. 3, 1907, 7th Annual Message. Public Papers of the Presidents-Containing Public Messages, Speeches & Statements of the President, (Wash., DC: U.S. Gov. Printing Office.)

33. Theodore Roosevelt. April 14, 1908, Special Message to the House of Representatives. Public Messages, Speeches & Statements of the President, (Wash., DC: U.S. Gov. Printing Office.)

34. Theodore Roosevelt. May 4, 1906, Special Message. Public Messages, Speeches & Statements of the President, (Wash., DC: U.S. Gov. Printing Office.)

35. Theodore Roosevelt. Dec. 3, 1906, 6th Annual Message. Public Messages, Speeches & Statements of the President, (Wash., DC: U.S. Gov. Printing Office.)

36. Theodore Roosevelt. Dec. 3, 1907, 7th Annual Message. Public Papers of the Presidents-Containing Public Messages, Speeches & Statements of the President, (Wash., DC: U.S. Gov. Printing Office.)

37. William Howard Taft. June 16, 1909, Message to the Senate. Public Papers of the Presidents-Containing Public Messages, Speeches & Statements of the President, (Wash., DC: U.S. Gov. Printing Office.)

38. 16th Amendment. United States Constitution, adopted 1913.

39. John Fitzgerald Kennedy. April 20, 1961, Special Message on Taxation, April 20, 1961. Public Papers of the Presidents-Containing Public Messages, Speeches & Statements of the President, (Wash., DC: U.S. Gov. Printing Office.)

40. Calvin Coolidge. May 31, 1926, Memorial Day, Arlington Cemetery. Calvin Coolidge, Foundations of the Republic - Speeches & Addresses (New York: Charles Scribner's Sons, 1926), pp. 429-437.

41. John Fitzgerald Kennedy. Feb. 6, 1961, Special Message on Gold & the Balance of Payments Deficit. Public Papers of the Presidents-Containing Public Messages, Speeches & Statements of the President, (Wash., DC: U.S. Gov. Printing Office.)

42. John Fitzgerald Kennedy. April 20, 1961, Special Message on Taxation, April 20, 1961. Public Papers of the Presidents-Containing Public Messages, Speeches & Statements of the President, (Wash., DC: U.S. Gov. Printing Office.)

43. John F. Kennedy. Nov. 20, 1962, Press Conference. Public Papers of the Presidents-Containing Public Messages, Speeches & Statements of the President, (Wash., DC: U.S. Gov. Printing Office.)

44. John F. Kennedy. Jan. 23, 1963, Special Message on Tax Reduction & Reform. Public Papers of the Presidents-Containing Public Messages, Speeches & Statements of the President, (Wash., DC: U.S. Gov. Printing Office.)

45. John Fitzgerald Kennedy. April 20, 1961, Special Message on Taxation, April 20, 1961. Public Papers of the Presidents-Containing Public Messages, Speeches & Statements of the President, (Wash., DC: U.S. Gov. Printing Office.)

46. John Fitzgerald Kennedy. Nov. 20, 1962, News Conference. Public Papers of the Presidents-Containing Public Messages, Speeches & Statements of the President, (Wash., DC: U.S. Gov. Printing Office.)

47. John Fitzgerald Kennedy. Jan. 24, 1963, Special Message on Tax Reduction & Reform. Public Papers of the Presidents-Containing Public Messages, Speeches & Statements of the President, (Wash., DC: U.S. Gov. Printing Office.)

48. John F. Kennedy. Feb. 2, 1961, Message on Economic Recovery. Public Papers of the Presidents-Containing Public Messages, Speeches & Statements of the President, (Wash., DC: U.S. Gov. Printing Office.)

49. John F. Kennedy. Feb. 1961, National Industrial Conference Board. Public Papers of the Presidents-Containing Public Messages, Speeches & Statements of the President, (Wash., DC: U.S. Gov. Printing Office.)

50. Thomas Jefferson. Dec. 15, 1802, 2nd Annual Message. James D. Richardson (U.S. Representative from Tennessee), ed., A Compilation of the Messages & Papers of the Presidents 1789-1897, 10 vols. (Wash., D.C.: U.S. Gov. Printing Office, published by Authority of Congress, 1897, 1899; Wash., D.C.: Bureau of Nat. Lit. & Art, 1789-1902, 11 vols., 1907, 1910), Vol. I, pp. 342-345.

51. John Fitzgerald Kennedy. Aug. 13, 1962, Radio & Television Report to the American People on the State of the National Economy. Public Papers of the Presidents-Containing Public Messages, Speeches & Statements of the President, (Wash., DC: U.S. Gov. Printing Office.)

52. John Fitzgerald Kennedy. Nov. 20, 1962, News Conference. Public Papers of the Presidents-Containing Public Messages, Speeches & Statements of the President, (Wash., DC: U.S. Gov. Printing Office.)

53. John Fitzgerald Kennedy. Feb. 6, 1961, Special Message on Gold & the Balance of Payments Deficit. Public Papers of the Presidents-Containing Public Messages, Speeches & Statements of the President, (Wash., DC: U.S. Gov. Printing Office.)

54. Noah Webster. 1832. History of the United States (New Haven: Durrie & Peck, 1832), pp. 307-308, para. 49. Stephen McDowell & Mark Beliles, 'The Providential Perspective' (Charlottesville, VA: The Providence Found., P.O. Box 6759, Charlottesville, Va. 22906, Jan.94), Vol. 9, No. 1, p. 6.

55. Ronald Wilson Reagan. Dec. 1, 1988, dinner honoring Representative Jack F. Kemp of New York. Frederick J. Ryan, Jr., ed., Ronald Reagan - The Wisdom & Humor of the Great Communicator (San Francisco: Collins Publishers, A Div. of Harper Collins Publ., 1995), pp. 82, 107.

57. Andrew Jackson. Dec. 5, 1836, 8th Annual Message. James D. Richardson (U.S. Representative from Tennessee), ed., A Compilation of the Messages & Papers of the Presidents 1789-1897, 10 vols. (Wash., D.C.: U.S. Gov. Printing Office, published by Authority of Congress, 1897, 1899; Wash., D.C.: Bureau of National Literature & Art, 1789-1902, 11 vols., 1907, 1910), Vol. II, pp. 236, 240-241, 243-244, 260.

58. John Fitzgerald Kennedy. Jan. 30, 1961, Annual Message on the State of the Union. Public Papers of the Presidents-Containing Public Messages, Speeches & Statements of the President, (Wash., DC: U.S. Gov. Printing Office.)

59. John Fitzgerald Kennedy. Feb. 2, 1961, Special Message - Program for Economic Recovery & Growth. Public Papers of the Presidents-Containing Public Messages, Speeches & Statements of the President, (Wash., DC: U.S. Gov. Printing Office.)

60. John Fitzgerald Kennedy. Feb. 6, 1961, Special Message on Gold & the Balance of Payments Deficit. Public Papers of the Presidents-Containing Public

Messages, Speeches & Statements of the President, (Wash., DC: U.S. Gov. Printing Office.)

61. John Fitzgerald Kennedy. Feb. 13, 1961, Luncheon Meeting of the National Industrial Conference Board. Public Papers of the Presidents-Containing Public Messages, Speeches & Statements of the President, (Wash., DC: U.S. Gov. Printing Office.)

62. John Fitzgerald Kennedy. Feb. 15, 1961, President's News Conference. Public Papers of the Presidents-Containing Public Messages, Speeches & Statements of the President, (Wash., DC: U.S. Gov. Printing Office.)

63. John Fitzgerald Kennedy. April 20, 1961, Special Message on Taxation. Public Papers of the Presidents-Containing Public Messages, Speeches & Statements of the President, (Wash., DC: U.S. Gov. Printing Office.)

64. John Fitzgerald Kennedy. May 16, 1961, Letter to Mrs. Alicia Patterson, Editor & Publisher of Newsday, Concerning the Nation's Response to the Cold War. Public Papers of the Presidents-Containing Public Messages, Speeches & Statements of the President, (Wash., DC: U.S. Gov. Printing Office.)

65. John Fitzgerald Kennedy. Jan. 11, 1962, Annual Message on the State of the Union. Public Papers of the Presidents-Containing Public Messages, Speeches & Statements of the President, (Wash., DC: U.S. Gov. Printing Office.)

66. John Fitzgerald Kennedy. Jan. 18, 1962, Annual Budget Message, Fiscal Year 1963. Public Papers of the Presidents-Containing Public Messages, Speeches & Statements of the President, (Wash., DC: U.S. Gov. Printing Office.)

67. John Fitzgerald Kennedy. Jan. 22, 1962, Message Presenting the President's First Economic Report (Published in 'Economic Report of the President, 1962'. Government Printing Office). Public Papers of the Presidents-Containing Public Messages, Speeches & Statements of the President, (Wash., DC: U.S. Gov. Printing Office.)

68. John Fitzgerald Kennedy. April 18, 1962, President's News Conference. Public Papers of the Presidents-Containing Public Messages, Speeches & Statements of the President, (Wash., DC: U.S. Gov. Printing Office.)

69. John Fitzgerald Kennedy. April 30, 1962, Address Before the United States Chamber of Commerce on Its 50th Anniversary. Public Papers of the Presidents-Containing Public Messages, Speeches & Statements of the President, (Wash., DC: U.S. Gov. Printing Office.)

70. John Fitzgerald Kennedy. May 8, 1962, Letter to the President of the Senate, the Honorable Lyndon B. Johnson, & to the Speaker of the House, the Honorable John W. McCormack, Concerning Standby Authority To Reduce Income Taxes. Public Papers of the Presidents-Containing Public Messages, Speeches & Statements of the President, (Wash., DC: U.S. Gov. Printing Office.)

71. John Fitzgerald Kennedy. June 7, 1962, President's News Conference. Public Papers of the Presidents-Containing Public Messages, Speeches & Statements of the President, (Wash., DC: U.S. Gov. Printing Office.)

72. John Fitzgerald Kennedy. June 14, 1962, President's 36th News Conference, held in the State Department Auditorium, 4pm Thurs. Public Papers of the Presidents-Containing Public Messages, Speeches & Statements of the President, (Wash., DC: U.S. Gov. Printing Office.)

73. John Fitzgerald Kennedy. July 6, 1962, Letter to David Rockefeller on the Balance of Payments Question. Public Papers of the Presidents-Containing Public Messages, Speeches & Statements of the President, (Wash., DC: U.S. Gov. Printing Office.)

74. John Fitzgerald Kennedy. Aug. 13, 1962, Radio & Television Report to the American People on the State of the National Economy. Public Papers of the Presidents-Containing Public Messages, Speeches & Statements of the President, (Wash., DC: U.S. Gov. Printing Office.)

75. John Fitzgerald Kennedy. Nov. 20, 1962, President's News Conference. Public Papers of the Presidents-Containing Public Messages, Speeches & Statements of the President, (Wash., DC: U.S. Gov. Printing Office.)

76. John Fitzgerald Kennedy. Jan. 14, 1963, Annual Message on the State of the Union. Public Papers of the Presidents-Containing Public Messages, Speeches & Statements of the President, (Wash., DC: U.S. Gov. Printing Office.)

77. John Fitzgerald Kennedy. Jan. 17, 1963, Annual Budget Message, Fiscal Year 1964. Public Papers of the Presidents-Containing Public Messages, Speeches & Statements of the President, (Wash., DC: U.S. Gov. Printing Office.)

78. John Fitzgerald Kennedy. Jan. 21, 1963, Annual Message: The Economic Report of the President. Public Papers of the Presidents-Containing Public Messages, Speeches & Statements of the President, (Wash., DC: U.S. Gov. Printing Office.)

79. John Fitzgerald Kennedy. Jan. 24, 1963, Special Message on Tax Reduction & Reform. (The complete message is printed in House Document 43, 88th Cong., 1st sess.). Public Papers of the Presidents-Containing Public Messages, Speeches & Statements of the President, (Wash., DC: U.S. Gov. Printing Office.)

80. John Fitzgerald Kennedy. Feb. 21, 1963, Special Message on the Needs of the Nation's Senior Citizens. Public Papers of the Presidents-Containing Public Messages, Speeches & Statements of the President, (Wash., DC: U.S. Gov. Printing Office.)

81. John Fitzgerald Kennedy. July 17, 1963, President's News Conference. Public Papers of the Presidents-Containing Public Messages, Speeches & Statements of the President, (Wash., DC: U.S. Gov. Printing Office.)

82. John Fitzgerald Kennedy. Sept. 18, 1963, Radio & Television Address on the Test Ban Treaty & the Tax Reduction Bill. Public Papers of the Presidents-Containing Public Messages, Speeches & Statements of the President, (Wash., DC: U.S. Gov. Printing Office.)

83. John Fitzgerald Kennedy. Nov. 18, 1963, President's Address & Question & Answer Period in Tampa Before the Florida Chamber of Commerce. Public

Papers of the Presidents-Containing Public Messages, Speeches & Statements of the President, (Wash., DC: U.S. Gov. Printing Office.)

84. John Fitzgerald Kennedy. Nov. 22, 1963, President's Remarks Prepared for Delivery at the Trade Mart in Dallas, Texas. Public Papers of the Presidents-Containing Public Messages, Speeches & Statements of the President, (Wash., DC: U.S. Gov. Printing Office.)

CPSIA information can be obtained
at www.ICGtesting.com
Printed in the USA
BVHW071204021021
617937BV00007B/637

9 780975 345504